Praise for *Nincompoopery*

[[Please save two pages for endorsements.]]

NINCOMPOOPERY

NINCOMPOOPERY

why
your customers
hate you—

and how to
fix it

John R. Brandt

HARPERCOLLINS
LEADERSHIP

AN IMPRINT OF HARPERCOLLINS

Published by HarperCollins Leadership, an imprint of HarperCollins Focus LLC.

Any internet addresses, phone numbers, or company or product information printed in this book are offered as a resource and are not intended in any way to be or to imply an endorsement by HarperCollins Leadership, nor does HarperCollins Leadership vouch for the existence, content, or services of these sites, phone numbers, companies, or products beyond the life of this book.

ISBN 978–1–4002–1368–9 (HC)
ISBN 978–1–4002–1458–7 (Ebook)

Library of Congress Cataloging-in-Publication Data
Library of Congress Control Number: 2018967935

Printed in the United States of America
19 20 21 22 23 LSC 10 9 8 7 6 5 4 3 2 1

For Emma and Aidan

To manage in turbulent times, therefore, means to face up to the new realities. It means starting out with the question: What is the world really like? rather than with assertions and assumptions that made sense only a few years ago.

—PETER F. DRUCKER, *MANAGING IN TURBULENT TIMES*

1. *The people running that company are a bunch of nincompoops!*
2. *Quit acting like a nincompoop, because I know you are smarter than that.*

—EXAMPLES OF *NINCOMPOOP* IN A SENTENCE, FROM *MERRIAM-WEBSTER* ONLINE

Contents

This book can be read in two ways:

1. If you want to understand why Nincompoopery is so prevalent today, start with the afterword, which explains the macro trends behind our current leadership predicament. This section offers background for the concepts in chapters 1 through 5. Go to page XX if you'd like to proceed this way.
2. If, however, your business is stuck *right now* in the throes of Nincompoopery, then skip the afterword for now. Why? Because if your company or career is metaphorically burning down, you don't need to know *how* the fire started, or *why* certain materials are so flammable: *you just need to put out the fire*. Quickly turn to chapter 1, and get to work!

Overview:

Are We Really Surrounded
by Nincompoops?

At almost every company we encounter (including, sometimes, our own), it can seem that we are surrounded by *nincompoops.* Things that should be easy are instead hard because, we believe, some nincompoop has forgotten to do his or her job, or didn't realize that there might be a better way to do the job, or couldn't care enough to even bother *thinking* about the job. We grow irritable as:

- Our phone call to our new bank is put on permanent hold because the *nincompoop* customer service representative (CSR) doesn't know how to solve an issue with the bank's website, and has no idea who else might. We're forced to call back later or visit a local branch.
- Our fancy coffee takes too long and ends up wrong anyway because a *nincompoop* barista asks questions (Medium

or dark roast? Room for cream?) but doesn't listen to our replies. We're forced to choose between delay or drinking something we didn't order in the first place.

- Our car doesn't get repaired because a *nincompoop* mechanic forgets to test a key component. We're forced to come back a second time to fix the problem—or to drive an unsafe vehicle.

In every instance, it seems, a nincompoop has wasted our time and cost their companies:

- labor, time, and materials (to rework the product or service they should have done right the first time);
- goodwill (you and I are cranky, not only at the supposed nincompoop but at a company numbskull-enough to hire him or her in the first place); and
- revenue and profit (disgruntled customers often reduce their spending with knuckleheaded companies, or desert them altogether).

In other words, nincompoops are not just irritating but incredibly expensive too. So why do the companies that seem to hire nincompoops tolerate them?

It's Not the Nincompoops— It's the Nincompoopery

Companies tolerate them because it's not the nincompoops—it's the Nincompoopery. Production failures, screw-ups, and faulty service aren't usually the fault of the supposed nincompoops with whom we're dealing but instead the Nincompoopery—i.e., the meta-foolishness—of the companies and systems in which they're forced to work. Ill-planned, outdated, or ludicrous organizational structures can turn even the most eager employee into a nincompoop, or at least force him or her to *seem* like one. Consider from the previous examples:

- If our bank had bothered to interview a sampling of new customers about what mattered most during a financial transition, they might have learned that in a commodity market—let's face it, most banks look pretty much alike—it's the simplicity of the transfer that matters most. A focus on making every aspect of the new customer experience easy to adopt and use, including training CSRs in common website issues, would not only save time and money but would also make customers more likely to recommend the new bank to others. The CSR wouldn't sound and feel like a nincompoop either.

- If the coffee shop had bothered to analyze its in-store traffic and workflow during peak demand periods, managers would know that errors start at the order stage, as overwhelmed clerks struggle to manage lengthy lines of barely awake, caffeine-deprived customers. The shop could then schedule more employees during predictable demand spikes and reconfigure order and brewing processes to speed delivery while slowing down human interactions. Customers would be happier, and baristas wouldn't feel like harried, defensive nincompoops.

- If the repair shop had bothered to train and trust the

mechanic on more than just technical skills—e.g., process improvement methodologies or the revenue and profit implications of his or her work—then he or she might have created an innovative way to review his or her work (a checklist, perhaps?) to prevent sloppy errors and wasted time. Satisfied customers would feel more confident in their repairs, and the mechanic wouldn't look or feel like a nincompoop.

It's important to note that in every instance above, there was no nincompoop problem; instead, there was a much larger Nincompoopery problem, in the way that each company failed to *understand*, *design*, and *deliver* customer value in ways that satisfied customers and boosted the bottom line. Even worse, the fix to each of these Nincompoopery problems was not unknowable or impossible but was, in fact, easily discernible and simple to implement. Yet in each case *nobody* in the company—not the employees, their managers, or senior leaders—seemed capable of overcoming *tradition*, *inertia*, and *apathy* to make simple changes that would save money and improve customer experience (and, ultimately, increase revenues and profits). Instead, like most companies (and most employees and leaders), they continued to do the same irritating things, in the same irritating ways, day after day, *despite* knowing better.

And while this sort of Nincompoopery is maddening and unfair to us as customers, it's perhaps even more maddening and unfair to the CSRs, mechanics, baristas, and other employees who are put into in positions *where they have no choice but to be seen as nincompoops.* This isn't to absolve nincompoop employees completely (they could complain, or suggest improvements, or quit), but it does mean that when Nincompoopery runs rampant, the *real* blockheads are the leaders and would-be leaders who don't put a stop to it—and who continue to squander money, time, employee devotion, and customer loyalty.

This book helps leaders put a stop to Nincompoopery, making their lives (and those of their customers and employees) immeasurably more fun and their companies measurably more profitable.

What's the Catch?

There's only one catch, but it's big: as simple as any *individual* Nincompoopery fixes may seem (survey your customers, hire more baristas, train the mechanic, etc.), fixing an *entire* organization's Nincompoopery problem is much harder, in part because being a leader itself (without being a nincompoop) is significantly more difficult today (see the afterword).

That's the bad news.

The good news is twofold:

1. An Anti-Nincompoopery plan is ready and waiting for you and your company.
2. You already know enough to get started.

This book—which includes examples from more than one hundred leaders and companies—will help with the rest.

How Can You Be So Sure?

A little background: I've been fascinated by how companies work—or don't—for more than thirty years. I've studied corporate performance (and, inevitably, corporate Nincompoopery) in three ways:

1. *As a practitioner*: I've been an employee, manager, turnaround leader, president, CEO, consultant, and entrepreneur in industries ranging from health care to media to consulting to greeting cards, among others. I've made most of the mistakes that you can make in each of those positions and have learned over thirty years to make fewer of them (i.e., to stop being such a bonehead).

2. *As a journalist*: I've been an award-winning business reporter, columnist, editor, and publisher for more than twenty years at a variety of magazines, including *IndustryWeek* and *Chief Executive*. I've had the privilege of interviewing an astounding number of really smart leaders, as well as an equally astounding number of nincompoops. Both taught me well.

3. *As a management researcher:* I've spent the last sixteen years as CEO of a global research firm, The MPI Group, which benchmarks the performances and practices of companies across a wide array of industries—from manufacturing to health care, from mining to high-tech, from beauty salons to pest control services. We focus on:

    - *identifying* high-performance companies and managers via hard metrics regarding performances and practices;

- *understanding* why and how these firms and executives outperform competitors via deep analysis of the data; and then
- *sharing* insights into the strategies, tactics, and best practices deployed by these high-performance organizations and leaders so that others can enjoy the same excellence and profitability (i.e., stop being or seeming like nincompoops or victims of corporate Nincompoopery).

I've learned many things over thirty years, but MPI has learned far more in its sixteen years. We've interviewed, studied, or surveyed executives at more than fifty thousand companies and business locations, analyzing more than ten million data points about corporate performance. We can tell you about performance and best practices in specific industries with astonishing granularity. For example, we know how leading manufacturers reduce work-in-progress (WIP) inventory or optimize operating equipment efficiency (OEE) in more than twenty industries; we know how much better or worse profit margins are on internet-enabled products in more than twenty industries; and we're happy to divulge the minimum number of hours you should train every employee, every year, if you want your company to be world-class, regardless of industry (forty hours). We've published thousands of pages of insights from this data, and I've given countless speeches and webinars on how leaders can improve their companies' performances in specific functions ranging from supply chain to operations to customer service to compliance . . . the list goes on and on.

And yet, that's not the whole story, or even the most important one. Because while a granular analysis of performance and activity is important at a process, department, or functional level, a company's *culture* is even more critical in determining organizational success or failure. And what we find, over and over, is that leaders of top-performing companies organize their cultures around three deceptively simple strategies—even as their doofus competitors ignore them.

1. **Innovation:** Are you developing, making, and delivering new value that meets customer needs at a pace faster than the competition? (See chapter 2)
2. **Talent:** Are you achieving competitive advantage by having superior systems in place to recruit, hire, develop, and retain the best talent? (See chapter 3)
3. **Process:** Are you recording annual productivity and quality gains that exceed those of competitors through an organization-wide commitment to continuous improvement? (See chapter 4)

These are *deceptively* simple strategies for three reasons, two good and one bad.

1. These strategies are readily available to every organization, big or small, in any sector. (*Good*)
2. If you and your peers are willing to think differently and work hard, the strategies aren't expensive to implement. (*Even better*)
3. Most organizations are rife with Nincompoopery, which deadens the souls of their employees (including, sometimes, you or me) and leads them (us) to act like nincompoops. To

wit, we get stuck in old ways of doing things; we convince ourselves that change would be impossible because nobody could fix such a nincompoopish company anyway; or we fret that even if we tried to lead a change, none of the nincompoops to whom we report or work with would listen. Really, we human beings are endlessly inventive in thinking of reasons why *not* to change ourselves, our companies, and our fates—in other words, we're really good at remaining nitwits and stuck in Nincompoopery. (*Not so good*)

Fortunately, it doesn't have to be this way (see chapter 5).

Why? Because among those fifty-thousand-plus companies and locations MPI studied (and the many more we didn't) are a significant number who have done *great* things, and almost every one of them did it when leaders organized their cultures around the three strategies laid out above. The single difference between those companies and yours is that at *some* point, *some* employee or *some* executive decided that he or she—and, by extension, the entire company—should stop acting like a hopeless victim of Nincompoopery (i.e., like a nincompoop or a bunch of nincompoops), and instead figure out a better way (as exemplified by the leaders and companies you'll meet in chapters 2, 3, 4, and 5).

That *some*body should be you.

And don't worry if you don't feel ready (you are), or qualified (you are), or confident that an Anti-Nincompoopery plan can fix your team, or location, or unit, or company (it will). Most leaders of high-performing companies doing great things had the same concerns, hesitations, and worries as they began their journeys toward personal and corporate leadership transformation. Yet once started, they found that they were already far more prepared than they ever imagined.

You will too.

Shall we begin?

CHAPTER 2

Innovation:

What Is Innovation, Anyway?

Innovation, Schminnovation

I have yet to meet the CEO who doesn't love innovation. In fact, the way most senior executives talk, innovation is right up there with champagne, *foie gras*, and year-end bonuses. The problem with innovation—at least in the way most nincompoop leaders invoke it, as a prayerful but mysterious mantra—is that while everybody *loves* it and nods enthusiastically when they hear its name whispered seductively, most people have little understanding of what innovation actually means.

In fact, when we hear syrupy words regarding innovation, they usually refer to a shiny new product or service that incorporates a major advance in technology—something like the Model T, or the iPhone, or maybe even the SpinBrush (the first low-cost, mass-market electric toothbrush). Innovations like these are exciting, they're game-changing, and they make for great magazine copy and video roll. They also fundamentally rearrange their industries as skyrocketing sales create massive profits that bestow commanding leads in market share—and often drive legacy companies out of business altogether.

It's no wonder, then, that we love this view of innovation, but it comes with an important caveat: this type of innovation is the most dangerous (and impractical, and nincompoopish) to pursue for most organizations, for three reasons.

Reason #1: Game-changing product or service innovation is rare in the grand scheme of things.

Of the 30,000 new consumer products launched each year, roughly 5 percent succeed.[1] Even worse, in a study of 1.5 million companies, just 9 percent were product or process innovators—meaning 91 percent weren't.[2]

Why the dismal statistics? Because it takes an *enormous* amount of money to find a truly revolutionary technology or product. Bringing a new prescription drug to market, for example, now costs nearly $2.6 *billion* and can take more than a decade.[3] Even a more prosaic new product like the SpinBrush, which entered the market priced at $5 each, required an upfront investment of $1.5 million (its inventors later sold it to Procter & Gamble for $475 million).[4] Most companies—especially the 60 percent of all US companies with less than $1 million in annual revenues[5]—will never be able to invest enough into research and development to deliver a revolutionary innovation based on technology, except through dumb luck. Unfortunately, the official First Rule of Innovation is: *Dumb luck is not strategy.*

Reason #2: Even if you are lucky enough to come up with a major technological innovation, your timing must be exactly *right.*

If your innovation is too *late*—after a competitor (e.g., Dumb Luck, Inc.) has already launched a similar new technology, even if that technology is inferior to yours—then you might as well not launch at all, unless you have buckets of money that you can spend out-marketing the Dumb Luckers or unless you're content to earn lower margins as "Oh-Yeah-That-Other-Brand."

Nike entered the wearable fitness tracker market in 2012 with its FuelBand, supported by a world-class brand, significant advertising, and enormous flair, including celebrity endorsements from Jimmy Fallon (impressive) and Lance Armstrong (oops). The FuelBand had functional advantages in tracking workouts but was bulky and—more importantly—didn't have the market share head start enjoyed by Fitbit (founded 2007, launched its Tracker in 2008) and Jawbone (founded 1999, launched its UP in 2011). The result? Despite Nike's marketing onslaught, Fitbit held 68 percent market share through 2013 versus 19 percent for Jawbone and just 10 percent for Nike. By April 2014—only two years after launch—Nike waved the white flag by laying off most of the FuelBand's development team.[6] The upshot: First-mover advantage counts for a lot, and you likely don't have it. Move faster next time. Or hope that you get dumbly luckier (see First Rule of Innovation).

If your innovation is too *early*—before customers see a clear need and payoff in adopting a new technology, which experience has taught them is likely to be painful, prolonged, and often unrewarding—you're in even more trouble. There's no lonelier feeling than trying to convince customers to buy something they've never heard of and don't understand, while commanding a premium price.

When the Segway was introduced, inventor Dean Kamen predicted sales of 10,000 per week—at $5,000 each. Unfortunately, as cool as a stand-up, self-balancing, motorized scooter may be, most people couldn't imagine why they needed one. Segway ended up lowering its prices and focusing mainly on police, industrial, and tourism markets—and sold 24,000 over the first five years (or roughly 2,576,000 fewer units—and about $13 *billion* less in revenue—than expected), at lower margins.[7] Remember that while evangelism has its rewards, they're usually redeemed far in the future, or after you're dead. Neither timeframe is helpful in delivering profits today, or in keeping your job (or company) alive next year.

Reason #3: No matter how enormous the sum you've invested in developing your revolutionary technology, you should plan on spending even more—way, way more—to launch and market it.

Business history is rife with examples of great products torpedoed by underfunded launch plans. Barnes & Noble launched the Nook e-reader in 2009, and by 2012 had partner investments of nearly $700 million from Microsoft and Pearson (a textbook publisher). Reviewers raved about the technology, but consumers followed the bigger brands and, more importantly, the marketing dollars of Apple (iPad) and Amazon (Kindle Fire), as well as offerings from Samsung and Google.[8] The Nook sadly illustrates the fallacy of the ever-popular (but always-nincompoopish) *Field of Dreams* product-launch strategy: "If we build it, they will buy." Um . . . no, they won't. In fact, they'll stay away in droves. If you don't have the money or talent to invest in a major launch, then you're better off selling your revolutionary technology to somebody who does.

All of which leads to the official Second Rule of Innovation: *Counting on a technology-related home run in product innovation is slightly better than waiting for dumb luck—but not much.*

We Are Our Own Worst Enemies in Preventing True Innovation

So what *do* we mean by innovation? It's helpful to step back from the outcome or result or end product—the innovation itself— and focus instead on the input or process or action involved, in other words, "to innovate." Why? Because too often in life and in business, we nitwittedly focus so intently on results—winning or losing, success or failure—that we lose sight of how to *achieve* the results we want. At home, we may desperately want to lose weight, plopping ourselves on the scale each morning in hopes that finally *this* new pill or *this* new diet will work, instead of focusing on the process of living a healthy lifestyle every day— eating in moderation, sleeping well, exercising, reducing stress. At the office, we call in our sales representatives and pretend that we're auditioning for a role in *Glengarry Glen Ross*, angrily demanding higher revenue goals without giving them new training or new tools to meet those targets. In both cases, we end up frustrated, discouraged, and despised (by ourselves or others), because our obsessive, panicked focus on results prevents us from asking the right questions about:

- what we really want (or what our customers really want);
- why we want it (or why our customers want it);
- how we might get it (or how we might provide it to customers); and
- how our lives will be different (better) if we achieve it (or how our customer's lives will be different (better) if they buy from us).

It's the same with innovation: when we take a deep breath and shift our focus *away* from how desperately we need a hit new product and *toward* how we might make our customers' lives easier (including ways that have nothing to do with our products or services), we start to think in creative new ways about what innovation really means.

It's Time to Rethink Innovation

The process of Innovation is "to innovate," which, according to *Merriam-Webster*, means:

to make changes; do something in a new way.[9]

The important thing to note in this definition is that it does not specifically refer to a new thing or product (although both could qualify). The definition describes doing things in new ways by having new ideas about how to do them—in other words, thinking differently. This is precisely what great leaders at great companies do in how they approach innovation: they think differently, with new ideas *about* innovation, driven by a deep understanding of what *specific* customers really value. What leaders at these organizations have learned, by the way, is that while customers love new products, services, and technologies, they often appreciate other components of customer value even more.

This is an important distinction and one that is often difficult to convey to Nincompoopery-trapped managers and employees who live in customer-free zones (e.g., executive row, the back office, the factory—actually, any location or position that doesn't have regular contact with real people who buy things from your organization). The traditional (i.e., outdated) way to think about customer value is that it involves something we make or do or offer—adding value to work in process, offering a product to an end-user, delivering services or information. All these activities can be components of customer value, but by themselves do not constitute customer value in its modern context.

Customer Perception of Value Has Shifted Dramatically

Connectivity and the resulting *relationship economy* have changed the way customers think about value. It's no accident that smartphones—which leverage wireless communication, access to the internet, and social media to connect us 24/7—have spread faster than almost any technology in history. The original telephone needed fifty years to move from 5 percent to 50 percent reach into US households; smartphones went from 5 percent to 40 percent in four years—*during the worst economic downturn in seventy years*.[10] Yet despite all the jokes, hand-wringing, and kvetching about how smartphones have made society and our personal lives worse—Thanksgiving dinners full of people posting grudges on tiny blue screens in their laps instead of arguing face-to-face—we love being connected with the larger world and in particular with each other. The anxiety that we as individuals sometimes feel about how technology is changing our *personal* relationships reflects a broader *societal* uncertainty about the new rules of acceptable behavior in a digital environment. What are the rules of attraction and interaction when we connect primarily via text and chat and finger swipes?

But at least we're thinking about how our personal relationships might evolve in a digital environment. At work, we've barely considered how these new technologies are altering our professional lives. That's a mistake, because the blizzard of connectivity we enjoy and endure each day profoundly impacts business culture, too, and changes how we manage our organizations, our careers, and our personal productivity.

These changes, in turn, are fundamentally transforming what customers want from us, and how they want innovative value to be delivered.

How Customers *Manage* Determines How (and Why) They *Buy*

To better understand customers today, let's walk back in time, into the dim mists of ancient personal productivity management (the early 1990s). Before the Apple Newton (1993) or PalmPilot (1997), before the email-enabled BlackBerry 850 (1999) or the iPhone (2007), early humankind relied upon perhaps the greatest organizational invention in history: the Legal Pad Method of

Management. Using this simple technique—jotting down every single task you could ever imagine doing if you had unlimited time, money, and bandwidth—cubicle-dwellers and CEOs alike could create lengthy, anxiety-producing lists that promised two things:

1. You could see, with absolute clarity, on a single sheet (or pad) of legal paper, all the obligations you'd successfully ignored for days, weeks, or months.
2. You could understand, with soul-crushing finality, the absolute impossibility of ever completing even a tiny fraction of the to-dos on your list.

But there was hope. Because if you were truly well-versed in the Legal Pad Method of Management you could, once a week or once a month, accidentally or on purpose, lose the entire list.

Why does this matter? Because, under official Legal Pad rules, when you recreated a lost list everything you didn't want to do magically vanished, as if the universe itself had granted forgiveness for all your past incompetence, procrastination, and laziness.

It was magnificent.

Today, however, we are beset by personal productivity technologies that *never* forget and are backed up in the cloud. This means that every morning, when we look into our smartphones or computers, we are immediately confronted by a tidal wave of overdue tasks, weeks-old emails, and unanswered texts that prove, beyond a reasonable doubt, what a loser each of us is—and how much each of us will never achieve in the future, because we can't even manage ourselves today.

It's a disaster.

The only consolation, such as it is, is that we are not alone. All of our peers and, more importantly for our purposes here, *all of our customers and clients feel exactly the same way.*

The impact of this change on how customers perceive value and what they ultimately buy is dramatic. In a business culture driven by electronic to-do lists that never go away, customers feel ever more stressed, harried, and short of time, at home and work. This is bad news for those of us who are marketers and sales representatives; when we seek to offer new products or services to distracted customers, they resist—some actively, some passively— learning about them because learning itself is just another task at the bottom of a list that's already too long. In fact, when we use traditional sales techniques—describing features and bene- fits, using open and closed probes—we think that customers are listening, but they've probably mentally left the building. Or, even worse, their blank stares mean that they can no longer see us, because in their eyes our heads have morphed into giant smart- phones. These customers stare mutely at our enormous blue-screen faces and ask themselves: *Is this person trying to add a task, or multiple tasks, to my to-do list? Or is this person offering to remove several tasks from my terrifying to-do list?*

This is critical. In industry after industry, customers are turn- ing to companies that focus on innovation through a simple lens: *How can we make our customers' lives simpler, happier, less stressed, and more productive, by removing or solving multiple issues with a single solution?* I learned this years ago from a friend who owns an advertising agency; he said that the secret behind all great marketing for professional services firms could be com- pressed into five words: *Me smart, make you rich.*

The secret to modern customer value requires six words: *Me smart, make you less stressed.*

Innovation Isn't Always What or Where You Think It Is

The wonderful, problematic, maddening, and exciting thing about innovation is how vastly different it is today than just a decade ago, based on how broadly customers now define value. It's imperative that we think creatively about what our customers really want from us, because it's often not what we imagine.

JD.com (formerly 360buy.com), an online retailer in China, offers an interesting example of how to rethink customer value. Imagine if during the downturn in 2007 and 2008—the period during which electronics retailer Circuit City entered its high-inventory, low-margin death spiral—you had been offered a chance to invest in an upstart electronics retailer. Would you have said yes? Most rational investors wouldn't. Yet 360buy. com moved aggressively into electronics retailing just before the global recession and kept going, achieving tremendous growth by rethinking customer value. How? By closing its stores and going online, but with a twist: a completely new take on service and delivery. Customers in major cities served by 360buy.com could now order televisions, stereo systems, or computers online by 11:00 a.m. and have the equipment delivered and installed by 6:00 p.m. the same day. If a customer missed the 11:00 a.m. deadline but ordered by 11:00 p.m., the equipment would be installed and delivered by 9:00 a.m. the next morning. And then, if a customer wasn't completely satisfied, 360buy.com promised that a representative would return within one hundred minutes to rectify the situation.[11]

Did it work? You judge: 360buy.com's online revenues grew from $12 million in 2005[12] to $18.2 billion (as JD.com) in 2013.[13]

These numbers are more than just a miracle of management and logistics; they're also the direct result of a fundamental shift in understanding what customers value. Leaders at 360buy.com realized that people don't really want to *purchase* a television or a sound system or a computer; what they really desire is to *watch* television or *listen* to music or *surf* the web. And they want to do so right now, with as little trouble and inconvenience as possible. Executives at 360buy.com flipped the retail model on its head, moving their sales focus away from products and toward stress-free delivery and enjoyment of those products.

An even more complex case study of value migration is Guinness. The company has grown dramatically in Ireland and around the globe since Sir Arthur Guinness founded the brewery in 1759, famously signing a nine thousand-year lease for forty-five Irish pounds a year. The brand's longevity (260 years and counting) is due to not only Extra Stout's unique black color and taste but also to innovative marketing—from memorable taglines (1929's "Guinness is good for you") to creative promotions (1954's launch of *The Guinness Book of Records*)[14] to clever circumventions of alcohol advertising restrictions (1983's "Guinness isn't good for you" campaign).[15] Yet despite worldwide expansion, Guinness's growth slowed in the firm's home market of Ireland in the late 1990s, actually declining by 3 percent in the second half of 2001.[16]

Why? An MBA would start with standard questions:

- *Has quality declined?* Unlikely: Guinness was (and is) still using the same recipe, in the same brewery, that customers have loved for more than two centuries.
- *Is the marketing budget not big enough?* Again, unlikely: As anyone who's been to Ireland could tell you, it's hard to turn around on the Emerald Isle without seeing a sign or advertisement encouraging you to drink Guinness.

In many ways, Guinness is beloved in its home market and emblematic of Irish culture. But if the beer is beloved, and marketing is doing all it can, what could possibly cause a slip in sales?

Guinness executives worried. What they found was this: they had a *relationship* issue. Not with each other or with their partners, of course, but with younger consumers. To twenty-year-olds, Guinness was the brand of old folks. These less experienced drinkers gravitated toward lighter beers (Heineken) or cocktails.[17]

At the same time, others felt that Guinness had forgotten its roots in Ireland; Murphy's Irish Stout, for instance, commissioned market research that found that while stout (the beverage) inspired images of local pubs and community—bringing family and friends together—Guinness advertising had positioned its own Extra Stout as a "graduation" beer for those with sophisticated palates. Murphy's launched a campaign to exploit this difference and ended up boosting sales nearly 2 percent.[18]

Guinness executives got the message: focus on developing a relationship with younger consumers, yes, but understand, too, that the brand doesn't stand for "stout," it stands for "community." That's hard enough, but how can a company effectively respond to a relationship issue? By increasing the advertising noise on an island already soaked in Guinness black and gold? (Hint:

23

Relationship issues, whether business or personal, are generally easier to solve with less noise, rather than more.)

Guinness chose a quieter path, seeking to transform the brand's relationship with younger drinkers in unconventional ways. The most visible part of this commitment was the creation of Guinness Storehouse in 2000, a renovation of part of the St. James's Gate Brewery. The Storehouse includes restaurants, bars, an art gallery, and spaces for meetings or events, as well as exhibits about how Guinness is made. (The coolest feature, though, is an atrium shaped like a pint glass; at the top, the circular Gravity Bar glows at night like the head on a well-poured Guinness.) Most importantly, Guinness made the Storehouse a must-visit destination by scheduling concerts, gallery openings, fashion shows, and private corporate events—as well as all Guinness employee and bartender training—to attract their target demographic audience.[19]

"Over the last twenty years," said Grainne Wafer, Guinness's global strategy and communications director, "we've been actively looking to the future and thinking about how we bring in the next generation of Guinness drinkers. There is a maturity to the people who come into Guinness, we do find that people tend to come into the brand in their mid-twenties. That's the area we focus on—guys and girls who are at their first job stage, who are progressing a bit more."[20]

The most fascinating aspect of the Guinness case study is that the company faced a problem that could not be solved by any of the traditional ways that MBAs are taught to consider. Only by doing deep research, and even deeper thinking, could the company's leaders understand the difference between what customers were really buying from Guinness (a sense of community) versus how they paid Guinness (for beer).

This is the key question for all of us who manage lines or departments or firms of any size: What do our customers *really* want from us?

That's where value now resides, no matter how we get paid for it.

Value Is Always Fundamentally Determined by the End User

Not so long ago, major corporations around the world conducted one of the greatest marketing scams ever perpetrated upon unsuspecting customers. Using fancy phrases such as *Total Quality Management (TQM)* and *ISO 9000-certified*, these companies advertised that the value of their products was their "high quality"—meaning, of course, *that the products actually worked as intended.*

This begs the question: Shouldn't they have worked all along?

Customers thought so, too, and wised up in a hurry (the new international quality standard, incidentally, approved by customers worldwide in a unanimous vote, is *ISO 20,000WHOCARES?*). Their collective response to quality claims in advertising was, in effect, (A) "Thank you for not selling us crap that doesn't work," and (B) in the words of a famous song, "Is that all there is?"[21]

Customers now expect us to provide quality—outstanding product performance and service delivery—as a minimally acceptable threshold to even be considered in a purchasing process. *This means that quality, though essential to value, is no longer a differentiating component of value.*

Customers want more.

Figuring out what "more" might mean, however, is harder than it sounds, and requires taking a step back in how we define and think about value.

First things first: It is a fundamental truth that value is always perceived by customers at the point of the end user—even if that end user is twenty process steps and four companies away from us (e.g., from supplier to manufacturer to distributor to retailer to end user). And if that end user can't *see* the value that we added to that product or service, *we did not create value*, regardless of how much time, effort, or money we invested in trying.

This harsh truth is why many of us own computers that say "Intel Inside," the tagline of one of the longest-running (twenty-eight-plus years and still going) and most successful marketing campaigns in history. When Intel launched the program in 1991, many consumers considered the semiconductor chip a commodity product, easily interchangeable, with price as a differentiating factor in determining value. In fact, to this day, the vast majority of consumers would struggle to explain how one semiconductor chip differs from another, or why they should prefer Brand A versus Brand B. Yet the "Intel Inside" campaign—supported by nearly two hundred original equipment manufacturers (OEMs) and massive investments in cooperative advertising—dramatically changed consumer perceptions. In 1992, the first full year of "Intel Inside," the company's sales rose by 63 percent. By 2001, Intel held the sixth most valuable brand *in the world*. All because the company's leaders understood that if end users (computer buyers) couldn't perceive the value they created—even if that value was only one component buried deep inside another company's product—they wouldn't believe that Intel deserved a premium for the value it delivered.[22]

Value Now Has More Facets than Ever

The good news is that we now have more ways than ever to deliver the "more" in "more value," which means you now have four Big Innovation Jobs.

Big Innovation Job #1: Leverage delivery and logistics for competitive advantage.

Customers have always wanted services and products to be delivered on time. But in an era when just-in-time deliveries are critical to organizations adopting lean management principles (66 percent of US manufacturers already use Lean,[23] and the methodology is rapidly making inroads into health care, insurance, and other industries), *precision delivery* is a differentiating component of value. If a customer has only limited inventories of a key part that you provide—or needs your service to delight their customers—and you screw up a promised delivery, they'll never forget you. But not in the way you hoped.

For most large and mid-sized businesses, the solution to improved delivery lies within, by improving measurement practices and operational processes both internally and externally. Plumbers Supply Company, a 250-employee distributor in Louisville, Kentucky, had an order fill rate of 95 percent, which seems impressive until you realize that missing even one item (much less five) out of a one-hundred-part order can bring an entire construction project to a dead stop. Customers were not happy. Plumbers Supply responded by adopting a lean improvement methodology (more on this in chapter 4) focused on a new measurement: 100 percent *complete order fill rate*. Did we ship everything the customer wanted, on time? The new metric uncovered a host of process problems (also known as hidden, slow-killing profit leaks) throughout the organization; with the help of a consultant, the company invested in three years of intense analysis and workflow changes. The result? A renewed customer focus and higher margins, driven by a 20 percent jump in productivity.[24]

All of which is fabulous, unless you don't have 250 employees, three years, and a consultant to improve delivery. In a truly small business it's different: you just have customers who love your organization's creative touch but still want things now, and aren't afraid to tell you where else they can buy them. In this situation you'll need a partner, likely one of the major shipping organizations (DHL, FedEx, US Postal Service, etc.) to offer value-added logistics. Beau-coup, an online retailer of personalized wedding favors, started in an apartment in 2002 and grew to $16 million in annual revenues in just ten years—in large part by making sure that excited (nervous) brides and grooms got their orders on time, with free delivery and returns, in partnership with UPS. "We are not in the business to miss events," says founder Polly Liu. "We use every service UPS offers to get products there on time. We have a guaranteed delivery date."[25]

How do you use delivery and logistics to separate your organization from the competition?

Big Innovation Job #2: Partner with customers by offering business expertise in creative new ways.

Total cost of ownership (TCO) used to refer to purchase price plus annual fees and maintenance. Now, however, customers conceive of it much more expansively, and include evaluations of such diverse factors as:

- How difficult is your organization to work with?
- How well do your management and information technology (IT) systems integrate with those of the customer?
- What business expertise, even if not directly related to your product or service, do you offer?

In short: Are you a good partner?

Don't kid yourself: this is terrifying stuff. It's hard enough to do great work or provide great products; being a great partner is even harder, but it does offer big opportunities for the brave.

The jet-engine industry has been a pioneer in rethinking partnership as a differentiating component of value. Engines are massively expensive (up to $35 million each) and are sold into a highly competitive market that keeps margins low. The *only* way to make money is selling parts and maintenance over the thirty-year life of the engine, but competition is just as keen here.

What to do? Executives at GE Aviation—aware that airlines don't really want to buy jet engines but just planes that fly—decided to stop selling engines altogether. Instead, GE sells "Power by the Hour," charging airlines thousands of dollars per engine-operating-hour (guaranteeing optimized TCO). This benefits both GE and the airline in the following ways.

- An enormous fixed cost for the airline becomes a variable cost, allowing for flexible responses to changes in flight supply and demand.

- The airline gains a partner (GE) dedicated to keeping the engines running and minimizing downtime.
- GE continuously gathers data on engine performance, spurring improvements in maintenance techniques and product design.
- GE eliminates competition for aftermarket parts and service (a strategic necessity, since by 2008 service represented 25 percent of GE Aviation revenues and 50 percent of profits).[26]

Other industries (like packaging machinery and computer service) are adopting similar models in which customers only buy the production or service time they need, while the manufacturer or service provider retains ownership of the equipment or process, even if that machinery or process is still on the customer's premises. How would your customers buy differently from you, if they could?

All of this is a terrific new business model if your organization is big enough. It takes millions (or, even better, billions) of dollars to finance equipment, staffing, and accounts payable for customers, and requires you to maintain sophisticated accounting and IT systems to track their usage and billing and . . . Oh, the hell with it: if you run a small company, this model may not work for you. Yet.

Except partnership doesn't have to involve vast sums of money and a break room full of MBAs. Smaller companies can be good partners by offering specialized expertise or other value, even if that know-how or help is initially unrelated to what the customer is buying. Green Tomato Cars, an eco-friendly taxi company, launched in London with four cabs and accidentally found a partner in BskyB (now Sky Limited), a British telecommunications company, when BskyB's then-CEO James Murdoch's chauffeur had the day off. Murdoch had heard of the service, and gave it a try. A gregarious driver convinced Murdoch to introduce Green Tomato to BskyB's procurement group, which led to the firm's first major contract.

Not surprisingly—given that even a 25 percent growth spike in fleet size since startup meant that Green Tomato still had only five cars—the firm struggled to meet demand from its behemoth client. But Green Tomato offered something valuable that BskyB wanted, quite apart from transportation: a way to make a visible commitment to environmental stewardship. BskyB stuck with its tiny partner,[27] and Green Tomato bloomed into a burgeoning business (since acquired by Transdev) with global ambitions.[28]

It's even easier for small companies to partner with other small or mid-sized companies. In these situations, building a deeper relationship can be as simple as asking: "We have a great [insert one: hiring/safety/training/etc.] program. Can we share that with you?"

The point isn't how much money you spend, but how much real connection (and resulting good will) you can create between your two organizations, at multiple levels, among a variety of departments and employees. Your best customers will recognize the long-term value that this type of partnership creates, which will reduce the importance of price in your negotiations with each other and prevent competitors from even getting in the door.

What are you doing to deepen your relationships with customers by offering expertise unrelated to your core product or service?

Big Innovation Job #3: Incorporate data and information into your value proposition.

Creatively collecting, analyzing, and sharing data with customers offers a significant opportunity to differentiate. This can be as easy as sharing data on trends or end markets, in ways both simple and complex. A small organization might host a quarterly lunch-and-learn on the local economy, while marketers at professional services organizations—accounting, consulting, and legal firms, among others—have long understood that the way to engage customers is *not* via technical discussions of arcane rules related to commodity services (like audits or tax preparation). Instead, they offer thought leadership and content marketing (free research and content designed to offer insights to clients while highlighting the firm's expertise regarding specific industries or issues).

Visit the website of any top-25 accounting firm (Deloitte, Ernst & Young, KPMG, PricewaterhouseCoopers, etc.) and you'll find digital acres of white papers, articles, newsletters, blogs, infographics, videos, and podcasts, each targeted at a mind-numbingly specific sub-industry. Not coincidentally, you'll find similar acres of thought leadership at most top-25 information technology providers (IBM, Microsoft, SAP, etc.), because leaders at these companies—acutely aware of how quickly today's innovative software can become tomorrow's cloud-based commodity—are trying desperately to recast their organizations as professional services firms that just happen to get paid for selling software.

The good news for small companies is that thanks to social media platforms such as Facebook, Instagram, Pinterest, and LinkedIn, thought leadership and content marketing are now affordable for anyone with creativity and chutzpah. AJ Bombers, a pair of Milwaukee-based burger restaurants, was an early adopter, with founder Joe Sorge using Twitter first as a no-cost market research tool to listen to customer feedback, and then as a megaphone to engage customers *en masse*. Diners loved the digital interaction so much that they began to scrawl their Twitter usernames on the restaurants' walls.

But Sorge didn't stop there. He deployed other social media to drive event-based revenue (an important component of profitability in the hospitality and retail industries). In just one example, the company arranged to have kayaks at the restaurant on Foursquare Day, so that customers could earn "I'm On A Boat!" badges. The Badge Party resulted in record revenues on a Friday followed by two near-record days of revenues on Saturday and Sunday, long after the event was over. The upshot? According to Sorge, once the company reached an online "critical mass" of customers (after about six months of dedicated effort), the restaurants saw revenue growth of 60 percent or more[29]—all due to social media.

Not bad for an upstart in a commodity (burger joint) business.

Yet thought leadership and content are just two ways—and not always innovative ones, given the flood of boring thought leadership and atrocious content marketing out there—to use data and information to differentiate value. A better path is to provide information to customers so that they can independently make better decisions about how to customize and use your organization's products or services, improving *their* outcomes (because solutions are tailored to their unique issues) and *your* profitability (because better information allows them to manage processes previously staffed by your company).

An interesting early example of this was Bush Boake Allen Inc (BBA), later acquired by International Flavors & Fragrances. BBA created specialty flavors for food manufacturers, which at the time was a lengthy process that involved back-and-forth between BBA and demanding customers ("Too smoky," perhaps followed by, "Not quite smoky enough." Argh.). Tedious as the process was, the math was even more depressing because

- BBA ate all development costs (customers only paid after they were completely happy with a new flavor), which could be as little as $1,000 for a small adjustment or $300,000 for a new bundle of flavors;
- only 15 percent of BBA-developed flavors reached a final evaluation phase with the client; and
- roughly 5 to 10 percent of BBA-developed flavors ever reached the market.

Not exactly a tasty proposition.

BBA fixed the process (and the math) by outsourcing flavor development *to their customers* by creating an online tool that allowed a customer to select a flavor profile from a database, adjust the formula to his or her preferences, and then send a new flavor to a machine (perhaps on-site) that creates a sample (sort of a high-end paint mixer for flavors). If the customer doesn't like the flavor ("Still too *#& smoky!"), he or she can change the formula and try again.[30] It was an elegant, customized solution that reduced development time and costs while simultaneously putting the customer in control *and* tying that customer to a proprietary solution. Brilliant, but . . .

It's also the kind of solution that is massively expensive and complex, and out of reach for most small companies—unless they use low-cost digital and social media to empower customers (like using Twitter to allow customers to vote on new product names). Even more exciting for small businesses is the opportunity to crowdsource new product ideas from the people who'll actually buy them. This technique is used extensively by larger firms; for example, Frito-Lay's "Do Us a Flavor" contest generated 3.8 million flavor suggestions on Facebook, 22.5 million Facebook site visits per week, a 12 percent bump in sales, and Sriracha as the winning flavor. Hmm.[31]

But this technique is even better suited for smaller companies. Madison Electric, a manufacturer of electrical products (conduits, fittings, etc.), launched its online Sparks Innovation Center to attract ideas from end users and inventors. Suggestions are reviewed by both an internal engineer and a group of local distributors, contractors, and electricians. Heavily promoted on Facebook, Twitter, LinkedIn, and the company's own blog, the program helped boost new product sales by 37 percent and overall sales by 17 percent. Rob Fisher, the director of marketing who launched the program, said: "It has enabled us to be relevant to our industry because we are releasing products that are validated by our customer because they were designed by our customer. It also makes us look like a leader because we are doing things that are outside of the box in our industry and that we are actually understanding the rise of the digital consumer. People know that we are the guys that release all the products designed by electricians."[32]

What information or new products would your customers use or buy if you asked them?

Big Innovation Job #4: Offer value or solution bundles.

We've already determined that customers are overwhelmed by massive to-do lists, whether electronic or legal pad in nature, and desperately want partners who can make those to-dos disappear. Here's the problem: most of their daunting lists have a series of *bundled* to-dos—a series of process tasks that together (might) solve a larger problem. An example might be: Our current batch of vendors stink, so I need to (A) generate a list of new vendors; (B) interview, research, and rank them all; (C) check with other departments to see if the new vendors meet quality and delivery standards; and . . . well . . . lunch is coming up, and now that I think about it, maybe our current vendors aren't so bad after all.

All of which means that *bundled* to-dos require *bundled* solutions, which are typically more lucrative than individual products and services (customers will happily pay more to see a bundle of problems vanish) but much harder to deliver because they demand broader capabilities. Large organizations have a distinct advantage in providing bundled solutions; Apple's success with the iPod, for example, relied less on technological wizardry (at the time, competitors had digital music players at least as good) than on its clout with music companies, which allowed it to secure digital music rights for the iTunes platform and create a bundled, portable music solution.

It's important to note, too, that a bundled solution isn't just throwing stuff in a bag and offering a volume discount; a Happy Meal from McDonald's might be a good deal—and may even include a toy that temporarily prevents whining in the back seat—but it doesn't solve a complex, multi-faceted problem in new ways.

A recent example of how to do this well is illustrated by an emerging trend in the health care industry: "owning the disease." In this scenario, an organization provides a full spectrum of care for patients with a chronic health condition, offering information, products (such as drugs or devices), and services (such as home health care aides) to improve outcomes. An early adopter of this strategy was Merck Serono, which launched an ambitious effort in the UK to manage metabolic and endocrine issues. The company introduced a new delivery method for human growth hormone—easypod, a wireless injection system that uploads usage data to an electronic health record—combined with screening and counseling services to create an end-to-end solution for patients. But Merck Serono didn't stop there; the company also revised its business model, agreeing to be compensated by the National Health Service (NHS), the UK's major payer, for the quality of outcomes instead of unit sales of products or services. Under this model, everybody wins: patient compliance and health care improve, NHS costs are reduced (interventions after noncompliance are far costlier than prevention), and Merck Serono's market share (and profits) rise.[33] What's not to like?

Unfortunately, you probably can't overhaul an *entire* health care delivery system, or any complex, multifaceted value issue, if you run a small business; you don't have the money, footprint, or technical expertise to provide an end-to-end solution. But you *can* do this Big Innovation Job by finding gaps in current value systems and bundling your new (or existing) product or service with another customer purchase to increase the value of *both*.

Thirstie and Drizly, for example, are among a group of startups focused on same-day (actually, same-hour) delivery of alcohol to customers in large cities such as New York and Los Angeles. Their niche? Customers who like ordering take-out food via smartphone for delivery but who couldn't get wine, beer, or cocktails with the same ease. The two companies partner with local liquor stores for inventory, then take orders from customers via their proprietary apps and websites. Customers find the new service intoxicating: Drizly launched in 2013 and topped $5 million in revenues in 2014; Thirstie launched in 2014 and projected revenues of more than $1.5 million in 2015.[34]

Where can your organization create new value by cutting your customer's to-do list in half—solving two, three, or ten of your customer's most irritating problems at once?

The Bad News: Customers Can't Tell You What They Want

Okay! You're on your way. You've studied the four Big Innovation Jobs; you know if your organization is large, small, or somewhere in between; and you're intimately familiar with your team's strengths and weaknesses. There are lots of ways that you can innovate your product or service; you just need to determine what your customers value most. How can you find out? By asking them, of course! Except . . .

They won't tell you. Or, more precisely, they *can't* tell you.

Why?

Steve Jobs said it best: "A lot of times, people don't know what they want until you show it to them."[35]

This, in a word, sucks. But it's completely understandable: In 1979, nobody knew that they needed a Sony Walkman; until then portable, hand-held music had required a transistor radio and broadcast music. The Walkman changed the paradigm by allowing individuals to listen to music on cassettes (and later, CDs) that *they* chose or recorded, at times convenient to *their* schedules (during a commute, perhaps). Eventually it transformed the consumption of music from a social interaction (concerts or shared broadcasts heard through speakers) to a private experience (listener-chosen content via headphones).[36] You could no more ask a customer in 1979 if he or she wanted a Walkman ("What's a Walkman?") than you could have asked in 1989 if he or she wanted a web browser ("Eyebrows? For a spider web? What?").

So what *can* you do?

You could spend enormous amounts of money on market research and focus groups to figure out what customers want—there's no lack of consultants willing to take your money—or you could spend very little and guess. Either way, though, you'll end up in the same place, facing the same two Big Customer Value questions.

Big Customer Value Question #1: What do our customers and competitors think *that they know about value in our industry, but is actually completely wrong?*

This is a tremendously important question, because much of the time we *and* our competitors *and* our customers are a collective bunch of chowderheads and assume that value is the same now as it has always been. This thinking prevents innovation, because we stop imagining what value *could be*, if we could abandon the received wisdom and complacent biases that plague every industry. Starwood Hotels faced this conundrum in the form of a bar of soap. Specifically, the bar in each room's shower, which costs a hotel four dollars or more per day, per room. Every hotel executive would love to replace these bars with bulk dispensers, except for one problem: customers say that they want bars of soap, not dispensers, because dispensers are associated with truck stops. So most hotels do nothing, and eat the loss.

Starwood tried a different approach by choosing to *ignore* its customers' wishes. Instead, the company loaded its Bliss spa products into fashionable new dispensers and sold the concept by promoting a message of hip but affordable travel. Customers loved the new experience; Starwood loved the new profitability. But neither could have happened without the courage of Starwood's leaders in forgetting decades' worth of surveys and feedback about what they, and their customers, thought constituted customer value.[37]

Small businesses actually have an advantage in answering this Big Customer Value question, because these organizations are typically founded and led by entrepreneurs with a passion for a particular industry or solution, as well as deep knowledge of specific customer segments and emerging trends that can obviate the need for expensive market research. Founded in 2008, UK-based Wool and the Gang (WATG) has grown into a twenty-five-person supplier of high-end knitting supplies and finished goods (scarves, sweaters, etc.) by upending what everybody thought they knew about knitters. Said cofounder Aurelie Popper: "[We wanted to] change the way knitting was perceived into something that was cool and sexy, not so grandma-ish."

WATG recast the traditional view of knitters by hosting knitting parties in bars; signing name designers to create hip patterns (more than four hundred) and finished goods; and encouraging customers to post their projects (in-progress or complete) on Instagram. More importantly, the company also reinvented the fashion supply chain. WATG holds only a limited inventory of finished goods and meets demand spikes via "Gang Makers"—three thousand knitters who purchase (at full price) materials for requested items and who then receive 78 percent of the item's final retail price (as much as $700 or more).

The result? Sales jumped 300 percent in 2014[38]—a number that persuaded Crowdcube investors to pledge more than £1 million ($1.5 million)[39] in 2015 to support expansion.[40]

What could you achieve if you could forget what everybody else (the nincompoops) think they know about value in your industry?

Big Customer Value Question #2: What problems do our customers experience in their everyday lives that we could solve, if only we knew about them?

I can't stress this enough: if your organization doesn't have a program in which *every* employee—from CEO to frontline worker—spends at least some time with a customer at least once per year, you cannot innovate. Period. This time, by the way, can't be spent pitching or selling or attending the big game together in your fancy loge. It has to be invested in working directly alongside the customer, in his or her workplace or home, observing how he or she operates in his or her own environment. This is the *only* way to identify nagging problems and new challenges that you can solve via innovation. Too many leaders rely solely on satisfaction surveys or net promoter scores to judge how well their organizations are doing with customers. It's nice, I suppose, to get a good grade from your customers on what you did *yesterday*, but how does that tell you what they might buy *tomorrow*—whether from you or a competitor?

Procter & Gamble (P&G), which spends nearly $2 billion annually on R&D,[41] has been a pioneer in working directly with customers. One example: in Mexico, the company's market share for Downy fabric softener stalled in the early 2000s, despite the fact that 90 percent of Mexican women reported using fabric softeners. Unsure how to improve sales in a lower-income demographic—households earning $215 to $970 per month comprised 60 percent of the country's population—executives were deployed to explore this target market as part of P&G's "Living It" program. Each manager—many of whom had grown up in more prosperous settings—lived, ate, and shopped for days with a typical low-income family, recording observations of their daily problems and challenges.

What they found was not so much a problem with Downy as it was with water itself—specifically, consistent access to water. Many lower-income city-dwellers have running water only intermittently; in rural areas, it's not unusual for lower-income women to carry buckets of water from pumps or wells. Few of these families, city or country, can afford automatic washing machines.

In short, laundry, though culturally important, is an overwhelming task in lower-income households.

This spurred P&G's "Aha!" moment. Downy's formulation at the time required a taxing six-step laundry process of:

- wash,
- rinse,
- rinse again,
- add softener,
- rinse, and
- (You've got to be kidding me) rinse again.

No wonder they had a hard time selling softener (and three extra process steps).

Using feedback from the "Living It" home-stays, P&G reformulated its softener in 2014 as Downy Single Rinse and cut the laundry process in half to:

- wash,
- add softener, and
- rinse.[42]

Consumers loved it immediately, saving both time and up to 50 percent of their water usage. P&G did well too; Downy sales rose 62 percent in the new formulation's first six months on the market.[43]

Executives at megacorporations aren't the only leaders who need to be reminded who their customers really are and what they really need. Big Bottom Market opened in 2011 to offer specialty foods and crafts, wine, and high-end casual breakfast and lunch dining in impossibly scenic Guerneville, California (located in Sonoma County on the Russian River). Seasonal business boomed—weekly sales to vacationing oenophiles, kayakers, and hikers reached $24,000 just two months after opening—but cratered soon after, dipping to $4,000 in November as tourists fled to jobs or warmer locales. Layoffs and impending bankruptcy forced the store's owners to rethink their winter survival strategy, which led to (Shock!) a realization that they might need to also consider the needs of *local customers*: the town's 6,500 permanent residents, as well as consumers in nearby towns.

Drastic and creative measures ensued: the average price of a bottle of wine in the store was slashed from nearly forty dollars to fifteen dollars; locally themed sandwiches, affordable dinner service, and catering were added to the menu; and the store's signature biscuit dough was offered as a frozen delicacy to the regional community via San Francisco's trendy Bi-Rite Market.[44] Customer service became a mantra: when a patron complained bitterly on Yelp about service related to a purchase of soap, cofounder Michael Volpatt contacted him and offered to ship his purchase to San Francisco, two hours away from Guerneville. When the customer didn't respond, Volpatt *drove* to his house and dropped off the soap, and collected $12.50 in the process.

"I told him that I'm really sorry that it happened," said Volpatt. "And I asked him for one favor. I asked him to make sure people knew about what we did."

The customer raised his rating of Big Bottom Market on Yelp to five stars.[45]

And Big Bottom survived.

How far would you go to live with customers to find out what they really need?

More importantly, where do you think your customers will look for new value and innovation this year? And how will you offer it to them?

Anti-Nincompoopery Planning: Innovation

Remember *This*.	Then Ask Yourself *This*!
Customers are more stressed than ever.	How can we make our customers' lives simpler, happier, less stressed, and more productive by removing or solving multiple issues with a single solution?
Big Innovation Job #1 *Leverage delivery and logistics for competitive advantage.*	How can we use delivery and logistics to separate ourselves from the competition?
Big Innovation Job #2 *Partner with customers by offering business expertise in creative new ways.*	How difficult is our organization to work with? How well do our management and information technology (IT) systems integrate with those of our customers? What business expertise, even if not directly related to our product or service, can we offer?
Big Innovation Job #3 *Incorporate data and information into your value proposition.*	What information or new products might our customers use or buy, if we simply asked them?
Big Innovation Job #4 *Offer value or solution bundles.*	Where can we create new value by cutting our customer's to-do list in half—solving two, three, or ten of their most irritating problems at once?
Big Customer Value Question #1 *What do our customers and competitors* think *that they know about value in our industry, but is actually completely wrong?*	What are the biases and received wisdom about customer value in our industry? What great value, service, or innovations do our customer enjoy in unrelated industries that they wish we would replicate in our industry?
Big Customer Value Question #2 *What problems do our customers experience in their everyday lives that we could solve, if only we knew about them?*	How can we make sure that every employee—from CEO to frontline worker—spends at least some time with a customer at least once per year?

CHAPTER 3

Talent:

Who's Going to Do All This Stuff?

Ah, Talent: How do we love thee? Let us count the ways:

1. You, our human capital, are our most precious asset! We remind you of this all the time, in newsletters and in our CEO's speeches, because we know you like that sort of thing. We're sensitive that way.

2. We also tell our customers that we graciously allow our most valuable assets (That's you again, Talent!) to walk out the door each night, because customers like that touchy-feely side of us too. We don't mention, of course, that we expect you to check your emails while you're gone and to do the same amount of work, whether you're on duty or not. For the same pay. Hey, it's good that we miss you, right?

3. We've learned that you're a little touchy about all the nin-compoop bosses we've assigned to you, so we're making up for it by officially relabeling you as "associates," not

employees. You'll still have to salute Mr. Nincompoop, but now you can pretend that you're his peer. Isn't that great?

4. And, well, there are so many other ways we adore you. Like . . . Whoa, look at the time! I know you've still got a lot to do, and you'd probably like to get back to it. Time is money, right? We've really enjoyed this little chat, though, and we should do it again soon. Raises? Oh, we can talk about that too. Got to go!

Is it any wonder that most of our employees are dazed, distracted, and disaffected?

It doesn't have to be this way. More importantly: It can't be this way, if you and your organization hope to do great things.

What Do We Really Mean by "Talent"?

Just as we did with innovation, let's start with the dictionary. According to *Merriam-Webster*, talent is:

> a special, often athletic, creative, or artistic aptitude:
> general intelligence or mental power: a person of talent,
> or a group of persons of talent in a field or activity.[1]

Fair enough. All of us know someone who can juggle or balance a spoon upon his or her nose; those are certainly *special aptitudes*, but not terribly useful for our purposes (unless, of course, your business is a carnival or circus, in which case these might be important interview criteria). In thinking about innovation, however—about creating new value for customers—the definition of talent is slightly different. Although it would certainly help if the people we hire had special abilities (X-ray vision or telekinesis, to move large crates in the warehouse), what we really need are people focused on creating value for others, using "special" abilities such as:

- brains,
- street smarts,
- empathy,
- curiosity,
- eagerness to learn,
- emotional intelligence,
- creativity,
- energy,
- focus,
- dedication,
- loyalty, to principles first, and then to people, and
- ability to play nicely with others (what your human resources department calls "collaboration").

Talent, then, collectively describes all the individual people—and they are individuals, not human capital, or pieces of a workforce, or assets—whom you hire, onboard, train, inspire, and reward to create new value for customers, shareholders, and, surprisingly enough, for themselves.

This isn't just more touchy-feely lingo, either; research tells us that creating innovative new value and great companies is possible only when you have the best talent. MPI research tells us that there are two factors that correlate most strongly with improved overall performance, in productivity and profits, regardless of industry.

1. How many hours of training do you provide annually to each employee? (Hint: More is better.)
2. How empowered are your employees? In other words, how broad and deep is their authority to make decisions that impact profitability? (Hint: More is better here too.)

It's not hard to understand. In a modern, developed economy, there are many business and management models from which to choose, but the only ones that work are those that stress decentralized control—putting decision-making authority close to customers and to the frontlines of work (e.g., production processes or customer service). Successful command-and-control management structures are now found only in organizations that deploy force (for example, military or police environments) or, for brief start-up periods, in rapidly developing economies (hiring and training large numbers of unskilled workers can be problematic without strict procedures and hierarchies). But the great and terrible thing about decentralized management is that frontline employees make thousands of decisions a day, and millions per year, that impact your customer relationships and drive your margins up or down.

Which begs the question: How smart, creative, and reliable do you want those employees to be?

You Only Have Three Jobs with Talent. Don't Screw Up.

This means that there's good news and bad news in the primacy of decentralized, non-hierarchical management structures. The good news is that you, as a leader (and non-nincompoop), now only have three Big Talent Jobs.

The bad news is that all three jobs are a much harder than they seem.

Big Talent Job #1: Hire well.

In one sense, this is basic self-preservation; if you make a mistake in hiring, not only will you end up with unhappy customers, irritated coworkers, and more work on your plate (fixing nincompoop mistakes, soothing ruffled feathers, writing an unfixable nincompoop's dreaded performance improvement plan), but you also have to look your Mistake in the eye, every day, and watch endless screw-ups until you fix it. As in, helping the Mistake to find a more appropriate career path, perhaps in a Nitwit Store. Or anywhere, really. But firing people, even Mistakes and Irredeemable Buffoons, no matter how deserving, is unpleasant work, and many leaders understandably shy away from it. In fact, if you have a modicum of decency, the idea of taking away someone's livelihood will cause you enormous angst, doubt, and pain. This is not something to be done lightly, quickly, or egotistically (*Hey, Mom, look how tough I am!*).

And yet Mistakes and Unfixable Dunderheads have to go.

And not just because they don't fit in, which may not be their fault, or how much they cost (CareerBuilder reports that

41 percent of US firms lost more than $25,000 from a bad hire in the last year),[2] but because they take up space, wages, and management time better spent on "A" players, the people who make customers' lives better, coworkers happier, and your own life easier. Unfortunately, some experts are forecasting an impending shortage of "A" players; according to Georgetown University's Center on Education and the Workforce, the United States faces a shortfall of some five million skilled workers by 2020.[3] Boston Consulting Group offered an even more dire prediction: by 2030, twenty-five major economies will face talent shortfalls that could collectively cost about $10 trillion in lost global GDP (about 10 percent of the world's 2013 GDP).[4]

The upshot: If you think it's hard to find talent now, just wait.

Big Talent Job #2: Train, train, train.

Finding great talent is only the opening ante in creating new value. Great firms mold, sharpen, and improve talent with training, and not just for technical skills. It's increasingly important to train for all the other skills that create great teams and a great work environment: competencies in communication, collaboration, and improvement methodologies are just a few. Lots of senior executives talk about the importance of culture to the success of their organizations but forget that each one of their employees (including him-or herself) was once a foot-stomping, tantrum-throwing three-year-old. Most of us, in at least part of our psyches, still are. And we were all raised differently, schooled differently, married and maybe divorced differently, managed or mismanaged differently; some better, some worse, and some awfully. This means that most, maybe all, of what we learned about relationships and teamwork and interaction and communication and collaboration was deeply imprinted (or ever-lastingly scarred) into us well before we arrived at our current companies and our current responsibilities. Is it any wonder that a ragged band of tempestuous three-year-olds, nominally grown into adults with suits and ties and skirts, intermittently treated both well and shabbily, might struggle with the notion of a common culture? Or even a common goal?

Evolved leaders understand that investments in training and culture aren't nice-to-haves but must-haves. In 2007, Boys & Girls Clubs of America (BGCA) faced a yawning skills gap due to a cycle of impending retirements. But the nonprofit, which coordinates activities for more than 1,100 local groups at more than 4,000 locations, transformed challenge into opportunity with a three-pronged strategy.

- First, BGCA developed an assessment process that measured fifty different components among all local leaders. BGCA analyzed the data and found that four of the fifty components correlated with significantly better performance:
  - ability to recruit an effective board;
  - skill in development of revenue strategies;
  - an "investor's mind-set" regarding the organization's future; and
  - leadership characterized by "tenacity and persistence."
- Next, BGCA created a leadership development system focused on the four components; more than 650 leaders from 250 locations went through the program.

- Finally, BGCA measured the performances of local groups with trained leaders versus those without trained leaders.[5]

The results were dramatic: Groups with trained leaders outperformed across the board, and the program as a whole generated a 300 percent return on investment. More importantly, BGCA estimated that if all local affiliates could have duplicated the feats of groups with trained leaders, overall BGCA revenues could have increased $100 million, boosting budgets (during the Great Recession, no less) at an average location by 2 or even 3 percent.[6]

Real training equals real money.

Or you could follow the example of an executive I met at a conference. I was mid-speech, extolling the virtues of training, when he stood up in the back of the room and said: "You know what? You're talking about skills and training. Well, I've heard all this before."

He paused, then continued. "Let me tell you what happened. We tried training, and we realized that we can't afford to train. You know why? Because every time we trained somebody, as soon as they got good, they left us for a job somewhere else. So we had to stop."

The room was silent.

And then—because this was, if nothing else, a lively group—another executive from a different company stood up, looked at me and then at the numbskull who couldn't afford training, and said:

"You know, sir, I have to tell you: that is the single best employee-retention strategy I've ever heard. Keep your employees so ignorant that nobody wants to hire them."

Big Talent Job #3: Get the hell out of the way.

If, and it's a big *if*, you do the first two talent-related jobs well, then the third job is a little easier: get lost. Because if you've:

- hired or retained the right individuals;
- given them the right training, skills, support, and technology; and
- set them up in the right decentralized management structure, with the right amount of education and authority to make decisions (i.e., lots), then . . .

. . . your new job (since you won't be fixing Mistakes or firing Irredeemable Chuckleheads) is to be less visible day-to-day, but to have more fun. Your new role will be to have *big* new conversations with customers, think *big* new thoughts, and to imagine *big* new things for your company.

Oh, and to invest the *big* new profits you're now earning.

Too Good to Be True?

You have a right to be skeptical. "Sure," you might say, "talent is important, but can you actually measure its impact?" After all, in our own careers, we've all suffered through meaningless training sessions, or endured Neanderthal managers, or watched incompetent human resource practices destroy the morale of coworkers. Yet we and most of our coworkers kept plugging away, and most of these companies survived, more or less. How much difference can better leadership and better management of talent really make?

It's an important question. Businesses in the United States spend in excess of $150 billion per year on employee learning, yet research indicates that 90 percent of its impact disappears within a year. Put another way, more than $135 billion is wasted annually on training that lasts barely longer than the sugar buzz from the session's donuts.[7] This waste, by the way, isn't so much due to the training itself but to our collective nincompoop (mostly non-existent) follow-up and measurement regarding new skills. Training at work is like learning in any other setting: without repetition, practice, support, testing, and reward, it doesn't last.

So why bother?

Because in modern decentralized management structures, with decision-making close to the customer, nothing matters more than how well our employees are trained, especially during what McKinsey & Company calls the "moment of truth."[8] This is the instant when there is an opportunity for something to go dramatically right with a customer, or, perhaps more often, immediately after something goes drastically wrong (an important order is lost in transit; a critical part fails; or a financial account is hacked).

How our company responds at that moment will shape our relationship with that customer forever.

That's not hyperbole. A study in Europe found that 87 percent of bank customers who had positive experiences during moments of truth (a check put on hold, a bank error, receiving financial advice) actually increased their share of wallet with the bank.[9]

Just as telling: 72 percent of customers who had negative experiences at those moments of truth downsized their relationships with the bank.[10]

It's important to define what constitutes a moment of truth. It's not a routine transaction; it's when stakes are higher—when a customer is emotionally invested in both the outcome and in being recognized as an individual.

In these moments, as evidenced by the bank study, the difference isn't *what* happens to the customers but *how* they are treated as it happens. Every long-lasting relationship, whether business, personal, or romantic, is fundamentally forged during times of crisis. It's at these moments—when people are nervous and hopeful, when plans unravel, when people are angry or disappointed—that we learn whom we can count on and whom we can't.

It's these moments, personally and professionally, that build or destroy trust.

It's hard enough to handle these moments well in our personal lives, when we have only ourselves to manage. At work we have to rely on our coworkers and employees. The only way that we create a difference at any individual customer's moment of truth is by the investment we make in talent, training, and culture. That difference, for good or ill, will determine our bottom lines for years to come.

Finding the *Right* Talent

Let's return to Big Talent Job #1: finding the people who will love your customers as much as you do; who will be as creative as you in taking care of them; who will selflessly devote themselves to you and to the rest of the team; and who will watch your bottom line as closely as your ex-spouse's divorce lawyer.

Good luck.

The reality is that it's really hard to find the right talent, in part because there's nobody just like you, who cares as much or in the same way as you do, for both better and worse. (It's a boring life if everybody thinks the same things.) But mostly it's hard to find the right people because they only become the right people after they've been hired the right way, trained the right way, and gained the right experience at your company. Great employees, and leaders for that matter, are made, not born.

Yet this doesn't mean that you can hire just anyone and then magically transform them into model employees.

So, who should you hire?

Skills and experience matter, of course, but many leaders focus too intently on résumés (in part because they don't trust their own judgment, or hope to avoid blame later if a hire goes wrong) and not enough on the character of whom they're interviewing. This may seem old-fashioned or vaguely inappropriate (who are we to assess someone else's character?), but when that moment of truth with a customer arrives and you're nowhere to be found, who do you want making decisions? Someone with a glittering curriculum vitae but no empathy or spine? Or someone less experienced but who cares desperately about doing the right thing?

Leading companies recruit for *smarts, diligence,* and *caring.* For more than forty years, Southwest Airlines' success—the company has made money forty-four years in a row[11] and transports more US passengers (upwards of 130 million) than any other carrier[12]—has been built on finding people with the right priorities. It's not easy: in 2015 alone, the company received nearly 300,000 applications, interviewed more than 100,000 candidates, and hired less than 7,000 employees (roughly 2 percent of all applicants).[13]

"We talk about hiring not for skills but three attributes," wrote Julie Weber, vice president of people at Southwest Airlines. "A warrior spirit (that is, a desire to excel, act with courage, persevere and innovate); a servant's heart (the ability to put others first, treat everyone with respect and proactively serve customers); and a fun-loving attitude (passion, joy, and an aversion to taking oneself too seriously.)" These character traits are reinforced by a management system (including 360-degree evaluations) that coaches for results and process (*how* you get results).[14]

Hiring for character is even more important at small companies; with a tiny team, everyone has to be willing to do any job that creates value for customers without regard to rank, tenure, or ego. A great example is the Special Care Center, a physician practice in Atlantic City, New Jersey, that focuses on managing the heath of a specialized group of patients: select union employees of local casinos and a hospital (AtlantiCare Medical Center), who have exceptionally high medical costs. Funded by a monthly per-patient fee, the Special Care Center offers same-day appointments (to cut down on emergency room visits), a social worker, and the practice's secret weapon: a staff of full-time health coaches, who meet with patients every two weeks (or even more often). Health coaches follow up on medication compliance, help with lifestyle changes (quitting smoking, beginning exercise or yoga, etc.), and, most importantly, offer encouragement and sympathetic ears to patients with chronic, often debilitating, medical issues.[15]

The results have been dramatic. These patients—among the costliest 10 percent of the union's members—reduced their health-care bills by 25 percent. But these expenses and lives couldn't have been improved without innovative hiring standards. Why? Because the health coaches don't usually have backgrounds in health care; instead, they've come from Sears, or Dunkin' Donuts, or the casinos themselves.[16]

"We recruit for attitude and train for skill," explained Dr. Rushika Fernandopulle, founder of the Center. "We don't recruit from health care. This kind of care requires a very different mind-set from usual care. For example, what is the answer for a patient who walks up to the front desk with a question? The answer is 'Yes.' 'Can I see a doctor?' 'Yes.' 'Can I get help making my ultrasound appointment?' 'Yes.' Healthcare trains people to say 'No' to patients."[17]

Fernandopulle means what he says: he dismissed half of his initial employees, including a physician, because they didn't embrace the Center's innovative approach to patient service.[18]

How different would your company be with the right employees? More importantly: What qualities would the right employees have?

Build a Talent Machine

It's incredibly hard to find the right talent, résumés aren't that useful, and we're supposed to somehow peer deeply enough into a job candidate's eyes (but not too deeply; that would be weird) to see his or her soul, so we can know if he or she has the right stuff to work for us.

Awesome. There's just that little problem of: How?

Fortunately, a number of pioneering companies (large and small) have developed new approaches. But all of them started by taking a step back from the hiring process and focusing instead on their overall goal: finding, developing, and leveraging talent who can create new value for customers, shareholders, and themselves.

This involves reflection and analysis (Whom do we need?), planning (How will we find, train, and deploy their skills?), and execution (How will we make sure that they're successful?).

In other words, designing and building a Talent Machine—a smooth-running process that continually finds, trains, supports, and rewards the best people. (Note: We'll talk a lot more about process in the next chapter.)

Hertz, a rental car firm with more than 11,000 locations in roughly 150 countries,[19] has invested an enormous amount of time, effort, and money into developing a Talent Machine. The company faced a major challenge in 2007: high voluntary turnover among new employees within their first ninety days (they quit) drove up hiring costs (it's expensive to keep finding new quitters), and also damaged service delivery and customer satisfaction. In a hypercompetitive industry—imagine having your rivals three feet away at the next counter—customer service failures lead to immediate lost sales and lagging long-term growth.[20]

Hertz executives needed to act.

Many companies would have redoubled recruiting efforts by offering incentives to employees for referrals, or by issuing stern warnings to local managers to be cuddlier with new employees (because "stern" and "cuddly" pair so well). Instead, Hertz hit the pause button and asked: What are our long-term recruitment goals?

That question led to the creation of Hertz's Global Talent Management Center of Expertise (GTM). The GTM team had two advantages over typical talent initiatives: the active endorsement and leadership of a senior executive (Vice President of Global

Talent Management Karl-Heinz Oehler) and a proactive, process-focused orientation. Instead of merely reacting to a recruitment problem, GTM staff worked with internal Six Sigma and Lean improvement experts to understand the *why* of the employee turnover issue—to uncover its root causes and to improve overall hiring effectiveness.[21]

After studying the problem, the GTM group established critical recruitment objectives, including:

- creation of consistent global processes, tools, and policies that remain sensitive to specific local needs;
- development of measurable targets such as recruitment effectiveness and turnover cost reduction; and
- redefinition of the recruiter's role from "seeker of warm bodies" to "strategic talent advisor."[22]

Outstanding goals, beautifully stated, but . . . nothing really ever happens without a plan (happy accidents don't count, or at least aren't worth counting upon). This is where Hertz separated itself from a thousand other companies with impressively named talent initiatives: the GTM team reinvented the company's entire approach and executed with rigor, across a four-step (what, where, how, who) recruitment life cycle:

1. **Plan**: Identify *what* you need (talent requirements across the organization).
2. **Attract**: Determine *where* you can find what you need (internally, externally via referral or social media, etc.).
3. **Assess and Select**: Establish *how* you'll decide among

candidates (build a consistent process that includes screening, interviews, evaluation criteria and tests, etc.).

4. **Offer and Onboarding:** Choose *who* you will hire and then make sure that they succeed (make the offers, welcome them to their new work home, schedule training, etc.).[23]

It's instructive that the most important innovations in Hertz's reinvention of recruitment happen before (Hey, let's plan ahead for what and who we need!) and after (Hey, let's help these newbies feel welcome and succeed!) the traditional hiring process (résumés, interviews, and background checks). Nobody likes to feel like a number or a cog in a factory; so even as Hertz built a better talent machine, it made sure that new hires didn't feel like processed meat as they moved through it. Instead, the company made visible its commitment to their long-term success.

But maybe your company doesn't do business in ten thousand locations. Or have any believable way to use the word *global* in the title of anything you do.

You can still hire better than your competitors do, even the big ones.

Pal's Sudden Service is a regional fast-food chain built on three core pillars: speed, accuracy, and talent. Based in Kingsport, Tennessee, Pal's, which offers take-out only (no sit-down meals) at twenty-six locations, is known for tasty burgers, fries, and shakes delivered with insane quickness. How fast?[24]

- You drive up, order directly with an employee at a window on one side of the Pal's building (average eighteen seconds per transaction).

- Then you steer to another window on the other side, where a different employee hands you a meal (average twelve seconds per transaction).[25]

Best of all, you get exactly what you ordered, because Pal's hands out the wrong food only once in every 3,600 orders. That's an error rate ten times better than the average fast-food chain, even as Pal's serves patrons four times faster than the second-quickest fast-food restaurant in the United States.[26]

Customers love it.

How does Pal's do it? With a rigorous focus on talent. First, like most successful companies, the company targets character in hiring; Pal's uses a home-grown, sixty-question assessment based on the attitudes and personality traits of successful Pal's employees. Job candidates agree or disagree with simple statements such as:

- "I think it is best to trust people you have just met."
- "Raising your voice may be one way to get someone to accept your point of view."[27]

Those who fit Pal's culture are hired but immediately enter 120 hours of training, and must be certified for each job they'll perform before they can work alone. Most importantly, training never ends; at every restaurant, every day, on every shift, a computer randomly selects up to four employees to take a re-certification quiz on the skills required for one of their jobs. Pass, and all is well. Fail, and the worker heads back to training.[28]

"People go out of calibration just like machines go out of calibration," explained Pal's CEO Thomas Crosby. "So we are always training, always teaching, always coaching. If you want people to succeed, you have to be willing to teach them."[29]

Not surprisingly, turnover among Pal's well-coached teams is absurdly low (a third of the fast-food average). Retention is even higher among restaurant managers; just seven have quit voluntarily in thirty-three years.[30]

Do your employees love your company, and you, this much?

Training Matters. But Culture Matters More.

We've already touched on the importance of training, and then training some more. It's no exaggeration to say that you can't train too much; MPI research finds that the minimum threshold of training for world-class competitiveness, regardless of industry, is forty hours per employee, per year. That's five times the amount of training at many companies (MPI research finds that most firms train eight hours or less per employee, per year). High-performing companies train even more, typically requiring sixty hours per employee, per year; award-winning organizations may offer as much as three hundred hours of training annually.

How many hours of training do you offer to employees?

And training at these high-performance or award-winning companies isn't limited to job-specific skills, either. They also train on communication skills, teamwork, collaboration, improvement methodologies (Lean, Six Sigma, etc.)—pretty much everything and anything you can imagine.

These companies also educate on topics you might not imagine, including financial literacy and business acumen. Why? First and foremost, because smarter is always better than not-as-smart; but also because education is integral to culture. A decentralized management structure requires much more from employees than mere job skills or fluency in communications; it demands initiative, a willingness to take action on behalf of customers, colleagues, and the bottom line to create value for all three.

The problem is that at most companies, especially smaller ones, details about the bottom line and profits are hidden from employees. This is usually rationalized by senior executives as a competitive necessity (*We can't let Dumb Luck, Inc. see our margins!*) but what it really means is that they don't trust their employees, as in:

1. *What if our employees tell our customers?*
2. *What if our employees find out how much money we're making?*

Gasp. Ouch. Except: Your employees aren't nincompoops (you got rid of the unfixable ones already). They know not to tell customers things like number 1. Regarding number 2: They already know that you're trying to make money. By not telling them *how much*, all you do is make them imagine secret rooms full of hundred-dollar bills that you swim through, occasionally stopping to sip champagne at a tiki bar made of old spreadsheets.

There's a better way, and it's vastly simpler and significantly less scary than most leaders think.

The problem and opportunity are neatly summarized in this quote from an executive at Federal Warehouse, a then-$35 million, 300-employee shipping and warehousing concern in East Peoria, Illinois, describing a difficult period in the firm's history: "The assumption [among employees] was that just because they were busy, they were making money. They had no clue that in a couple of our locations, we had actually lost a significant amount of money in the year prior."[31]

The big question, of course, is: Why didn't employees know that the locations were losing money?

You already know the big answer: nobody told them.

Why? Because at most companies, for all our pious pronouncements about the value of our employees; for all our genuflection at the altar of Talent; for all our soulful whispers about how we want our workers to be our partners . . . we don't really treat them as partners. In fact, we often treat them as the exact opposite of partners: enemies, saboteurs, malingerers, complainers, whiners . . . basically, nincompoops.

Is it any wonder they, and we, so often dread coming to work?

Consider, instead, how you would treat a business partner. You'd share information. You'd share decision-making. And, most important of all: you'd share the rewards of your joint success.

Yet only 7 percent of private companies share financial data with all employees. And a staggering 76 percent share no financial information with employees.[32]

It comes down to respect and fairness, and most of us fail the test.

I've had the privilege and pleasure of visiting lots of firms, factories, and facilities, good and bad, over the years. Most of the employees and leaders at these organizations were thoughtful, well-intentioned people, with firm commitments to doing the right thing for their customers, companies, and colleagues. And yet I repeatedly heard a similar, sad story that more often than not foreshadowed extended mediocrity and misery. Perhaps you've heard or lived a similar tale. It goes something like this:

Enthusiastic Leader: "We have a terrific employee [choose one: involvement, engagement, activation] strategy! It's called the People [Working Together, Matter, First] Program!"

Me (or You): "Great! How does it work?"

Enthusiastic Leader: "If employees work 20 percent harder this year, we're going to give them each a T-shirt and a pizza party in January!"

Me (or You): "Wow."

This is, of course, the dumbest deal in history, and nobody in their right mind would accept it or offer it to a partner. But managers keep serving it up year after year, like a cold slab of meatloaf from three weeks ago. And smart employees keep pushing it away, like the stinky leftover it is.

Federal Warehouse chose a different menu. This firm adopted open-book management, which is a leadership strategy that shares financial information, decision-making, and rewards with employees. The theory behind this methodology is that if you hire the right people, train them the right way, give them the right (i.e., complete) access to all financial and operations data, and offer the right incentive, you can then delegate nearly all management to them, because they'll act like owners.[33]

If only it were that simple.

Unfortunately, one of the dirty little secrets of the American educational system is that we don't teach economics, business, or finance very well. We're all familiar with the ghastly workforce statistics about illiteracy and innumeracy in the United States:

• Illiteracy: 32 million Americans (14 percent of the total

population) can't read; another 21 percent read below a
fifth-grade level.[34]

- Innumeracy: Only 32 percent of high school students in
  the class of 2011 were "proficient" in math (which means
  that 68 percent weren't).[35]

Awful. Yet as bad as those numbers are, financial literacy
rates are even worse. Some 43 percent of Americans can't pass a
rudimentary financial test with questions such as "Suppose you
need to borrow $100. Which is the lower amount to pay back:
$105 or $100 plus 3 percent?" (The correct answer is $100 plus
3 percent. I won't tell anyone you asked.)[36]

But here's the rub: if you can't calculate simple interest, how
can you evaluate return on investment (ROI)? Or measure productivity improvements? What use, really, is an income statement
or a balance sheet to someone who's never been taught to recon-
cile a checking account?

More to the point: How can you, as a leader, possibly delegate
management to employees who can't differentiate margins and
profits from expenses and losses?

The answer is simple: education.

Finding the right people lays the foundation of success.
Delivering the right training erects the framework for success.
But offering the right education—about what it means to run a
business, about how to do the right thing even when it's not the
easy thing—builds the house in which long-term success can live.

That's why in Federal Warehouse's new program, each
employee started his or her career with a week of education on
open-book management and a detailed introduction to the company's financial statements. This crash course in business was

supported by monthly finance reviews with all employees and regular reports distributed throughout the company.[37]

Yet it's not enough to simply understand the drivers of financial success—the processes that create new value for customers and margins for the company. An employee also has to be motivated to leverage and improve those drivers. At Federal, motivation came from an innovative, three-stage incentive program:

- *Stage 1:* Before anything else, the company had to earn a fair return for shareholders. They invested and took on financial risk; they got paid first.
- *Stage 2:* After shareholders were compensated, 40 percent of every dollar of profit went into an incentive pool. Employees participated in the pool based on the performance of Federal as a whole versus budgeted profit (one-third of bonus pay) and that of their respective business units (two-thirds of bonus pay).
- *Stage 3:* Let's call this the "Wow" stage. If profits exceeded budget, 50 percent of every additional dollar of profit went into the pool.[38]

Federal paid out $385,000 in bonuses the first year and $443,000 the next year.[39]

That's a lot of money for a relatively small company. But it's dwarfed by what Federal got in return:

- Workers' compensation costs dropped from $625,000 to $350,000.
- Damage claims fell from 1.2 percent of sales (roughly $420,000) to 0.75 percent (roughly $263,000).

- Net income tripled in the program's first year and rose another 30 percent the next year.

All this happened without new products, technologies, or investments. The only thing that changed was culture—how Federal viewed, educated, and trusted its employees. Treated at last like partners, they acted like partners, and everybody made more money.

Best of all, empowering and rewarding workers to act on your behalf works regardless of your company's size or industry:

- It works for mid-sized companies (Federal Warehouse).
- It works for bigger companies such New Belgium Brewing, the nation's fourth largest craft brewery (their best-known beer is Fat Tire Amber Ale).[40] Founded in 1991, the Fort Collins, Colorado-based company requires financial training for all new hires; reviews results in monthly staff meetings;[41] and includes all employees in its annual strategic retreat.[42] This pays off in ways large and small; in just one example, two employees recommended elimination of twelve-bottle dividers, improving the company's sustainability (150 tons of paper no longer needed) and bottom line (costs reduced by $280,000).[43]
- It also works for the smallest of companies, such as Waltham, Massachusetts-based A Yard & A Half Landscaping, where founder Eileen Michaels reviews the P&L statement in detail each month with eighteen employees (in both English and Spanish). Workers offer suggestions on how to improve efficiency and profits; small bonuses are awarded weekly to those who create new value for customers or the company.[44]

The model works so well for A Yard & A Half, in fact, that the company was named one of *Inc.* magazine's "Top Small Company Workplaces in 2010" (alongside the New York Jets and Patagonia, among others),[45] and then became an employee-owned cooperative in 2014.[46]

How long can you afford (financially and emotionally) to keep managing everything by yourself?

More importantly, how will you find, train, educate, reward, and retain the best people to help you?

Anti-Nincompoopery Planning: Talent

Remember *This*.	Then Ask Yourself *This*!
In decentralized management structures, with decision-making close to the customer, nothing matters more than how well our employees are trained, especially during what McKinsey & Company calls the "moment of truth."[47]	How smart, creative, and reliable do you want your employees to be?
Big Talent Job #1 *Hire well.*	How will we evaluate the talent we have and find the new talent we need?
Big Talent Job #2 *Train, train, train.*	How many hours do we train each employee annually? Do we train only for technical skills, or do we include other skills—communications, collaboration, improvement methodologies, etc.—that create great teams and a great work environment?

Big Talent Job #3 *Get the hell out of the way.*	How we can set up our employees in the right decentralized management structure, with the right training, and the right authority to make decisions (i.e., lots)?
Leading companies recruit for *smarts, diligence,* and *caring.*	How different would your company be with the right employees? More importantly: What qualities would the right employees have?
Great companies build a Talent Machine, based on reflection and analysis, planning, and execution.	Who do we need? How will we find, train, and deploy their skills? How will we make sure that they're successful throughout their careers?
Training matters, but culture and education matter more.	How will you create a culture in which employees are treated like partners, because information, decision-making, and the rewards of success are shared with them?

CHAPTER 4

Process:

Hey, Let's Talk Process! Wait . . .

Where Are You Going? Come Back!

Sad but true: there's no faster way to clear space at a cocktail party than to announce, "Hey, we're doing something really interesting at work to improve our processes with [insert one: Lean, Six Sigma, quality, ISO, theory of constraints]."

Which is too bad, because process is how you'll actually profit from all the time, effort, and money you've invested in innovation and talent.

It's not hard to understand why process gets a bad rap. After all, innovation is fun! (Who doesn't want to get paid for thinking up crazy new stuff?) Talent is even more fun! (Who doesn't want to work with smart, motivated, and kind human beings?)

But process, the hard work of figuring out how to make your products faster, cheaper, and higher quality or your service faster, cheaper, and less irritating . . . Well, really: process is pretty much the spinach or broccoli of the strategy world. Or Brussels sprouts.

Basically, any vegetable that you don't like but that you know contains vitamins, antioxidants, and fiber critical to your health and to, um, keeping things moving.

And yet there's no faster way to improve your bottom line (and your ability to sleep at night) than to do something really interesting to improve processes at work with [insert one: Lean, Six Sigma, quality, ISO, theory of constraints].

Just don't be a nincompoop and talk about it at cocktail parties.

Process Equals Profits

Why does process—and the ability to intelligently document, analyze, and improve connected processes that deliver (or kill) customer value—matter so much? Let's start, as we did with innovation and talent, with a standard definition of process:

a series of actions or operations conducing to an end[1]

This is what process *is*: the way that you get things done, or, more to our purposes, how you create value for customers. And since we're interested in creating more customer value (and higher profits for you), the next question is obvious: Where in your business can you improve processes to deliver more customer value?

Alas: This isn't as easy as it sounds. When Ford managers standardized production of the Model T—training workers to specialize, automating simple tasks, and speeding assembly time from twelve days to under three hours—they found eighty-four process steps.[2] What a difference a century makes: today, even

small businesses have hundreds if not thousands of internal processes to get things done, from taking customer orders, logging
inventory and processing invoices to figuring out who's going to
mop the store tonight. Larger, more complex companies have a
geometrically higher number of interconnected processes (from
tens of thousands to tens of millions) as they coordinate suppliers,
employees, production lines, administrative departments, remote
facilities, distributors, and customers into a value machine that
efficiently and profitably delivers product, service, and satisfaction to customers.

The very idea of improving all these processes individually,
much less connecting them more efficiently, is overwhelming if
not headache-inducing. Add in methodologies or buzzwords like
Lean or *Six Sigma* or *theory of constraints* or *reengineering*, and
your eyeballs may be at risk if sharp objects are nearby.

That's why the guy at the cocktail party backed away so
quickly when you mentioned process improvement. And it's the
reason he and thousands of other nincompoopish would-be leaders purposely avoid thinking about it at work or in the businesses
they own.

It doesn't have to be this way.

You can create an organizational structure that consistently
delivers customer value and profit. How? By shifting your focus
away from the narrow specifics of how your company currently
manages individual tasks, and instead documenting the broad
processes across your entire organization, no matter how large or
small, that actually deliver value to your customers.

Look at Your Company Through Your Customer's Eyes

At MPI, we use the graphic shown in the Process Flowchart figure to show how processes typically fit together to create value (and profits) *from a customer's point of view*:

As you can see, we believe that a company has seven fundamental processes that can deliver value to a customer:

- **Research and Development (R&D):** Imagining, innovating, and designing great new products and services that customers can't wait to buy.
- **Procurement:** Finding and sourcing all the materials, components, supplies, talent, and technology required to create great products and services.
- **Administration:** All the boring but incredibly important back-office stuff that allows for the creation of great products and services (for example, finance, human resources, and maintenance).
- **Logistics:** Coordinating shipments of all the stuff you procured to the right places (your office, store, plant, etc.), and then delivering great products and services to customers, with as little stress as possible.
- **Sales and Marketing:** Making customers aware that you have great products and services, and then helping them to purchase them in ways that create new value for them.
- **Production and Performance:** Building great products and services with quality and speed.
- **Service and Support:** Staying with customers after the sale to make sure that great products and services do what they're supposed to do, and make your customers' businesses more profitable or their lives better.

There are three important things about this graphic:

1. Each of these overall functions is represented from a customer's point of view rather than in a more traditional organizational chart with boxes, lines, and arrows showing internal departments. This is critical, because most of

our companies aren't really organized around the needs of our customers but rather for our own convenience. Need proof? Look at a list of departments or job titles within your company, and then imagine asking a customer how each of those departments or job titles makes the customer's life better. At most companies, large or small, your customer will struggle to answer or to have any idea how a "senior analyst-channel analytics" or a "director of first impressions" creates new value. This is a huge problem not just for customers but for your company too. Employees who feel isolated from customers—and from the process of creating value for them—tend to invest time, effort, and budget into things that make their own lives easier rather than the lives of your customers. By focusing on broad processes from a customer's perspective instead of idiosyncratic organizational structures, this chart forces you and your employees to think about how individual activities create (or destroy) customer value.

2. Just as importantly, the functions in the graphic are represented in a continuous circle, rather than with boxes and lines connecting them to various executive vice presidents (EVPs) or subdepartments. Why? Because in high-performance organizations, each of these functions influences and improves all the other functions too. For example, service and support employees don't just fix customer equipment, or solve customer billing or delivery issues; they also gather data on what customers like and don't like about current product or service offerings, including what customers want in future products or services. Service and support then delivers this data to

R&D, which uses it to create next-generation products and services.

3. Your company or industry may look slightly different. Or you may think differently about how customer value is created in your business; perhaps you think there are five broad customer value-creation processes, or six, or eight. It doesn't matter, and you are welcome to adjust the graphic and the concepts in any way that suits your company. The important thing is that you have some rubric or diagram or concept with which you map value creation. I encourage you to take a moment right now and make a couple of notes on the graph for how your business differs.

Now the hard work, and the profits, begin. Look at your annotated diagram and ask yourself three questions:

- At which of these processes is our company great?
- At which of these processes is our company okay or sort-of-okay?
- At which of these processes is our company ridiculously terrible?

Be brutally honest in answering these questions, because even if you aren't, your customers will be, whether by telling you directly or by quietly switching to competitors. (These silent defectors kill your bottom line: it's five to twenty-five times more expensive to find a new customer than to retain an unhappy one.)[3] And no matter how bad you think you may be at one or two of these processes, console yourself with this truth: no company is great at everything. In fact, most companies are great or good at one or two of these value-creation processes; okay to sort-of-okay at three or four; and truly awful at least one or two—damaging customer value, customer retention, and profit margins.

Excel, Improve, and Fix—or Kill

Now's your chance to be a leader. With your diagram analysis, you've just given yourself three Big Process Jobs (we'll talk about how to do these jobs shortly).

Big Process Job #1: Fix or kill.

Start with what you you're terrible at, because every day that you ignore these value-creation processes, you're driving customers away and putting your company at risk. This will be at once the worst and the best job you'll ever have. It's the worst job because you'll have to focus on Nincompoopery and failures— including your own in letting the situation evolve or linger—and because your choices will be stark and distasteful. You will have to change the process; or change (improve or remove) the people managing the process; or get rid of the process altogether, by finding someone else to do it for you (outsourcing) or quitting it altogether if you can (exiting that product or service or process). This is the best job, too, because nothing feels quite so good as a long-term problem that's finally been eliminated. But remember: you're doing this job first not because it's most important, but because it's most urgent; it's as if your house needs upgrades or repairs, but your garage is *on fire*. In the long run, the upgrades and repairs to the house will create more value, but a garage fire will spread and destroy everything. So be brave, be quick, and be done with it. You have more important jobs waiting.

Big Process Job #2: Improve.

Next, move on to what you're okay or only sort-of-okay at. Spend the bulk of your time on improving these activities; even if you only get marginally better, you'll stop irritating your customers quite as much, which will keep them focused on why you're so great in the first place.

Big Process Job #3: Excel.

Finally, don't forget to spend time on what you're great at. This is the reason that you have a business or job at all and is why your customers or bosses love you. Invest at least as much time here as you do on your terrible failures, by focusing on figuring out how (A) you got great at this activity in the first place and (B) how you can become even greater (we'll cover this shortly).

Big Process Job #1—fixing what's terrible—is, paradoxically, the easiest of the three jobs. Why? Because (A) you probably already intuitively know some of what needs to be changed (e.g., Phil in accounting is an Unreachable Halfwit and has to go); (B) there's typically no disagreement between you and your bosses or partners about the fact that something has to be done, sooner rather than later; and (C) your downside is extremely limited because you're already terrible at whatever this process is. Even if your first, quick solution isn't perfect, it's still likely to be an improvement. Even more important, your effort here will demonstrate to customers that their pain matters to you, and that you are trying to be more responsive in meeting their needs—or, at least, are trying to irritate them less.

Big Process Jobs #2 and #3 are much tougher, however, and will take longer. Why? In part because you're already okay, sort-of-okay, or great at these tasks, so there's less room for improvement to begin with, and incremental gains will be that much harder to achieve. But you'll also need to move more carefully (slowly) than you did in in fixing the terrible stuff, because you face tremendous risk if you screw things up during an unsuccessful improvement initiative (the last thing you want to do is transform a process that's okay, sort-of-okay, or great into something terrible, losing customers in the process). At the same time, Big Process Jobs #2 and #3 also require a level of data granularity rarely available in most small-or mid-sized companies, or even in larger ones (especially on a department-, function-, or customer-specific basis). For example: Do you know how much it costs to fulfill a customer order? Most executives or business owners have only a vague idea—a rough guess at what it takes to pick and pack a few stock-keeping units (SKUs), or to load a thingamajig on a pallet, or to send a service rep to a customer's business or house—and completely overlook costs that should be allocated to each order to calculate profitability, including:

- Order receipt costs
  - Call center costs
  - Invoice processing costs
- Storage costs
  - Rent per square foot
  - Financing for inventory
  - Warehouse overhead
- Material costs related to fulfillment
  - Packaging supplies

- Unbilled shipping or transportation expenses
- Direct and indirect labor
- Management
- Etc., etc.

These costs vary dramatically by industry and company, but they also differ by customer (Does the customer order small or large volumes? Pay on-time or late? Complain or reject orders? Require additional, unpaid customization or rework? Reschedule service calls at the last minute?). These differences can significantly impact profitability, yet few companies calculate profit and loss (P&L) statements for individual customers, or even for major customer segments of their market.

Stop Shooting Yourself in the Foot

But wait: it gets worse.

Flimsy data and haphazard analysis of processes not only damage short-term profitability but long-term survivability, because executives with mistaken assumptions about how much value is being created in a given process usually make even *bigger* mistakes in investing for the future. Let's stay with the example above, the (deceptively simple) cost of order fulfillment. Imagine a CEO or senior executive starting a discussion with you about marketing:

> **Executive:** "We're putting in a new customer relationship management (CRM) system."
> **You:** "Awesome! Why do you want to do that?"

Executive: "Because we want to touch our customers
more often."

You: "Awesome again! But tell me: How much does it
cost you every time you get an order from a specific
customer?"

Executive: [Awkward silence, followed by either] (A)
"It's around [number guessed at on the spot]," or (B)
"[general industry benchmark, typically five, ten, or
twenty years old]."

This is no way to run a business, because if your operation is
like most companies, you have some customers that you should
not touch more often. In fact, you probably have at least a few
that you should *not* touch with a ten-foot pole. Why? Because if
you ran customer-specific P&Ls, you would find that these block-
head losers consume resources and time vastly out of proportion
to the margin that they contribute to the bottom line. This may
be one reason that the failure rates for CRM projects, even after
fifteen-plus years of widespread adoption, still hover between 30
percent[4] and 63 percent,[5] depending on how success is defined.

I once heard the CEO of a small manufacturing firm describe
how he managed a particularly difficult customer (a price-obsessed
whale who demanded 35 percent of the company's effort, but con-
tributed only 5 percent of overall profits). He took his customer
to a nice lunch, thanked him for his business, and then fired him
by offering the names of three of the CEO's competitors.

That's good, evil fun—just think about all the annoyance
your problem customer will inflict on rivals—but it takes guts and
probably a CEO title as well (Who else can tell a big customer to
go to hell?). The story's ending is instructive, however: the CEO's

customer returned six months later at a higher price and at an appropriate margin.

None of which would have happened if the CEO hadn't run the numbers and analyzed his processes.

Do You Measure Up?

There are literally thousands of metrics you can use to monitor current performance and your improvement effort. (But don't do that, you only need five to seven for each process. You'll go crazy otherwise.) Here are a few to consider for each value-creation process.[6]

Research & Development

- Percentage of new products launched on-time/on-budget
- Percentage of products developed as an integrated customer approach
- Customer satisfaction/retention rates
- New product sales/profits as a percentage of annual sales/ profits
- Right First Time, On Time (RFTOT) at each design process step
- Current total cost versus potential total cost

Procurement

- Raw material and component lead times/inventory turns
- Percentage of suppliers certified to your standards of operation
- Expedited shipments as a percentage of all shipments

- Cash-to-cash cycle
- Right First Time, On Time (RFTOT) at each supplier management process step
- Current total cost versus potential total cost

Administration

- Return on Invested Capital (ROIC)/Return on Assets (ROA)
- Labor turnover/absenteeism rates
- Accounts Receivable (AR)/Accounts Payable (AP) aging
- OSHA rates/safety
- Right First Time, On Time (RFTOT) at each administrative process step
- Current total cost versus potential total cost

Logistics

- Order fill rate/accuracy/cost
- Customer delivery lead time
- Perfect order rate (perfect deliveries ÷ total deliveries)
- Total inventory turn rate
- Right First Time, On Time (RFTOT) at each warehouse process step
- Current total cost versus potential total cost

Sales & Marketing

- Market share growth/customer retention rates
- Same-customer sales/profit change
- Sales-to-cash cycle
- Forecasting accuracy

- Right First Time, On Time (RFTOT) at each sales and marketing process step
- Current total cost versus potential total cost

Production & Performance

- First-pass yield/quality to customers
- Cycle time improvement
- Productivity per employee, per labor hour, or per asset (choose best measure)
- Customer satisfaction/ retention rates
- Right First Time, On Time (RFTOT) at each production process step
- Current total cost versus potential total cost

Service & Support

- Problems resolved as a percentage of contracts received
- Service contract/aftermarket sales as a percentage of total sales
- Warranty costs
- Customer satisfaction/retention rates
- Right First Time, On Time (RFTOT) at each service and support process step
- Current total cost versus potential total cost

But I Don't Have Detailed Numbers!

It would be lovely to have precise numbers on each process available online in a slick business-intelligence, big-data dashboard, or downloaded as a beautiful color-coded spreadsheet, complete with historical trend analyses. And if you work at a large, techno-logically proficient company with a well-established improvement methodology, a few of these magical numbers may already exist. In health care, for instance, process improvement initiatives can leverage a wealth of patient data to literally save lives. In just one example, an initiative of the American Heart Association, American College of Cardiology, and other groups focused on reducing door-to-balloon (D2B) times—the period between arrival of a heart attack victim at an emergency room and cor-onary angioplasty—to ninety minutes or less (the gold standard for lower mortality). More than one thousand hospitals signed up for "D2B: An Alliance for Quality" in its first six years, tracking data and sharing best practices. Across the United States, sub-ninety-minute D2B times rose from 72 percent of patients in 2007 to 94 percent by 2011.[7]

If you have one of these rich troves of data with relatively simple access, use it. God bless, and kudos to you. Unfortunately for the rest of us, this level of precision is unattainable anytime soon; hoping or waiting for it will only stall our efforts to get better. We'll have to think differently.

In other words, we'll have to make SWAGs (Scientific Wild-Ass Guesses) at the numbers and what to do next, in five steps.

SWAG Step #1: Start by choosing a customer value-creation process and mapping it. This can be as complicated and detailed as you like. Entire books have been written about various flavors of value-stream or-process mapping, and some value-stream maps extend the lengths of entire hallways, but my vote is for simpler and quicker. Make a drawing with a block for each key step (the fewer the better) in this particular customer value-creation process (for an example, see the "SWAG-gering Your Way to Greatness" sidebar).

Line Number	Value Creation Step 1	?	Value Creation Step 2	?	Value Creation Step 3
1	*Quality* rate: _____ percent		*Quality* rate: _____ percent		*Quality* rate: _____ percent
2	*Quality* plus (+)/minus (-) rating: _____ percent	T	*Quality* plus (+)/minus (-) rating: _____ percent		*Quality* plus (+)/minus (-) rating: _____ percent
3	*Process time:* _____ seconds/ minutes/ hours/etc.		*Process time:* _____ seconds/ minutes/ hours/etc.		*Process time:* _____ seconds/ minutes/ hours/etc.
4	*Process time* plus (+)/minus (-) rating: _____ percent		*Process time* plus (+)/minus (-) rating: _____ percent		*Process time* plus (+)/minus (-) rating: _____ percent
5	*Total time:* _____ seconds/ minutes/ hours/etc.		*Total time:* _____ seconds/ minutes/ hours/etc.		*Total time:* _____ seconds/ minutes/ hours/etc.
6	*Total time* plus (+)/minus (-) rating: _____ percent		*Total time* plus (+)/minus (-) rating: _____ percent		*Total time* plus (+)/minus (-) rating: _____ percent
7	*Net value* plus (+)/minus (-) rating (add lines 2, 4, and 6) = _____		*Net value* plus (+)/minus (-) rating (add lines 2, 4, and 6) = _____		*Net value* plus (+)/minus (-) rating (add lines 2, 4, and 6) = _____

SWAG Step #2: Now measure, calculate, or SWAG the three most important metrics for each key process step:

- *Quality* (line 1): What percentage of the actions at this step are high-enough quality to move the next step (in other words, the percentage of actions that, after completion, do not require extra work)? (For a service, the action doesn't need be redone; for a product, it doesn't need to be scrapped or reworked.) This metric will tell you how efficient your process is in creating quality products or services (or, conversely, how much wasted effort and material that an inefficient process generates).
- *Process time* (line 3): How long does this step take *for this action only*, not counting lead times or waiting times for other actions to occur (in other words, not counting the time waiting for other steps to be completed, or for more information or inventory to be delivered)? This step will tell you how fast or slow the process step is in creating a service or product.
- *Total time* (line 5): How long does this step take *including* all those lead times and waiting times for other actions that we excluded from process time (in other words, the time waiting for other steps to be completed, or for more information or inventory to be delivered)? This step will tell you how much delay and waste that other steps and actions (or inactions) impose upon this process step.

SWAG Step #3: Next, we're going to shamelessly steal (that is, benchmark) the sports analysis concept of plus/minus ratings. In basketball, for instance, a plus/minus rating measures the value of a player by calculating how many more (+) or less (-) points a team scores/gives up when that player is on the court. You are going to do something analogous by estimating how much better (+) or worse (-) you are, as a percentage, than an average competitor in creating and producing customer value for each key process step (the blocks you just scribbled down). You'll do this by looking at metrics typically associated with each process (see "Do You Measure Up?" sidebar), and comparing them to industry benchmarks (when available). Although some data—both for your company and for your industry in general—will be readily available, other data either won't exist or would take too much money and effort to calculate or collect. SWAG at those numbers; you're trying to improve your business quickly, not calculate the precise mass of a Higgs boson (it's about 125 GeV, if anybody asks).[8] What you want is a SWAG for each key step (for example, our service is roughly 20 percent slower than our competitors, or we launch about 10 percent more new products every three years). This will tell you where you're outperforming the competition and where you're falling behind. Jot your plus (+) and minus (-) SWAG percentages for quality, process time, and total time on lines 2, 4, and 6.

SWAG Step #4: Add lines 2, 4, and 6.

SWAG Step #5: *Voilà!* Based on SWAGs, you've created a simple chart that shows you exactly where your customer value-creation problems (also known as opportunities for improvement) for this process are. Now you can prioritize all the lowest (positive or negative) net customer-value margins for improvement efforts, and begin asking why you lag behind competitors in those steps, after one final step.

- Ask your customers if what you're about to do really matters to them!

SWAG-gering Your Way to Greatness

Value-stream or-process mapping can seem complicated, but it doesn't need to be. Let's imagine that we've become the managers of Nincompoopery Baristas, Inc.—the coffee shop that irritated us so badly in the Introduction by getting our venti cappuccino wrong—and do a quick analysis of their flawed order process.

Nincompoopery Baristas, Inc. Order Process

To further simplify our example, let's focus just on the first step—the order, which consists of interaction and data entry.

First, we'll measure how many orders we get wrong, perhaps by simply tracking how many customers complain in a given hour or shift. We find that during busy periods such as the morning rush, 4 percent of our orders are incorrect, for a 96 percent quality rate.

1. Quality rate: 96 percent

That doesn't seem bad, until our research (online, perhaps, or maybe just by going to a rival coffee shop and counting complaints) reveals that our average competitors only make mistakes on 2 percent of orders during those same periods. At Nincompoopery, *we're 100 percent worse.*

2. Quality plus (+)/minus (-) rating:-100 percent

Next, we measure how long it takes for the actual order to occur. We time the *order* interaction (not the waiting-in-line or payment times) between a Nincompoopery Barista and a customer during the same hour or shift. We find the average order time is 32 seconds.

3. Process time: 32 seconds

Much to our relief, our research on process time among our competitors finds that they have roughly the same performance at 31 seconds. At Nincompoopery, we're still 3 percent worse, but close.

4. Process time plus (+)/minus (-) rating:-3 percent

Finally, we measure total time—from the moment a customer steps into line at Nincompoopery Baristas until their order is recorded (but before payment). We discover that during busy periods, the average total time (including waiting in line, waiting for the cashier/clerk to come back from getting more coffee cups, etc.) is 8.5 minutes. This means that even though the order takes only 32 seconds in process time, it requires another 7 minutes and 58 seconds in *wasted time* (in other words, nothing is happening).

5. Total time: 8.5 minutes

Alas, at our competitors, total time during these periods averages only 4.5 minutes. At Nincompoopery, we are 89 percent *worse.*

6. Total time plus (+)/minus (-) rating:-89 percent

Adding lines 2, 4, and 6, we find that Nincompoopery has a combined net value plus/minus rating of-392.

7. Net Value plus (+)/minus (-) rating (add lines 2, 4, and 6) =-192

In short: *we are terrible at this process step.* The-192 isn't a percentage, but it is a dramatic shorthand method for highlighting the fact that we are irritating customers and killing our bottom line. Why? Because even if irritated customers don't abandon us, we're so much slower than our competitors that we can only serve half as many customers, irritated or not. That's half as much revenue and half as much marginal profit.

This is how businesses die.

But we can fix it.

Why? Because the value of this exercise is not in the numbers themselves (they're SWAGs, after all) but in how the numbers focus our thinking and our powers of observation. If we use this terrible grade on our terrible management of this process as a wake-up call, we and our team can start asking the magic question *why* about all of our terrible processes, over and over, and start our journey toward improving them. For example:

- *Why* is our quality rate 100 percent worse than our competitors'? Are Nincompoopery Baristas' staff undertrained? Is our menu overcomplicated?
- *Why* is our process time slightly slower than our competitors'? Is our counter arrangement clumsy or illogical? Do we need a faster order-entry technology or system?
- *Why* is our total time so much worse than our competitors'? Do they have more staff during busy periods? Do they allow text or email orders?

Asking all the *why* questions you can think of and fixing all the nin-compoopish reasons you discover is how your processes (and your business) will get better.

Validate, Validate, Validate

We've already established that you and your team are not nin-compoops and are more than smart enough to run this business, function, or department. You've done your analysis and you're SWAG-gering all over the place. But before you invest time, effort, and money into improving one of your customer-value processes, do yourself a favor and *ask your customers* if this will make a difference. Because if the idea is to improve customer value, then customers must value what you improve. And—smart and thorough though you are—it's simply impossible to know with certainty what customers want in improved processes without talking to them.

Ten Feet and Ten Seconds to Success

A terrific example of this is AT&T. Since you probably don't work in the mobile phone industry but probably have seen lots of cell network ads on television, you might imagine that the most important factor in customer satisfaction with various providers (Verizon, Sprint, T-Mobile, AT&T, etc.) is the strength of the network itself, or the variety of smartphones and tablets offered at its stores, or perhaps special pricing or deals.

Not even close.

According to AT&T research, overall customer satisfaction is most influenced by the way a customer is treated at its retail store. In fact, the single biggest driver of whether a customer will recommend AT&T to others is how well or poorly that customer is greeted in the first ten feet and ten seconds after he or she enters the store. This is an amazing insight, but even more impressive is how AT&T reconfigured its in-store processes to leverage that insight into improved satisfaction and loyalty among the thousands of customers who enter its stores each month. More specifically, AT&T developed a rigorous training and measurement program for associates that focuses on seven key process steps (six interpersonal, one technological) for making customers feel welcome:

Step 1: A friendly handshake.

Step 2: A smile.

Step 3: Make eye contact.

Step 4: Offer your name. "Hi, I'm _____."

Step 5: Ask politely for the customer's name.

Step 6: Ask why the customer is visiting the store.

Step 7: Enter customer data—name, description (clothing, for example: *navy blue suit*, or *purple jacket*), and reason for visit—into a system that displays a list of waiting customers in order of arrival (this is seen by customers as a fair way to allocate service in a crowded store).

That's a well-designed process for greeting anyone, in any context; I can imagine it being useful in teaching kindergartners (or even some adults) how to be polite in new social situations. Yet this isn't just good etiquette; it's good business too. Customers not only feel welcome, they feel *known*, because the personal data entered into the system is used by the next associate to greet the customer with both a name ("Hi, Lisa") and familiarity with the customer's issue ("I hear you want a new phone").

The numbers bear this out. Because of all this customer arrival and service data, AT&T knows exactly how long each person has waited to be served in its stores. This allowed the company to ask a simple question of two separate focus groups of customers, all of whom had waited precisely two minutes for service: "How many minutes do you think you waited until someone served you?"

The first group of customers (none of whom were greeted with the seven-step process within ten seconds of arrival) guessed that they had waited as much as five or six minutes before being served, or near three times as long as it actually took.

But the second group of customers (all of whom were greeted within ten seconds) correctly estimated that they had waited about two minutes. Not surprisingly, they were generally happier with the overall experience too.[9]

Let's be clear: warmly greeting customers is no substitute for a solid network, a broad selection of products, and competitive pricing. But in a rapidly commoditizing industry (in other words, a sector in which everybody's products and prices start to look the same), companies must improve processes in ways that differentiate themselves. AT&T figured out how to delight customers by delivering a human touch missing in other retail settings and was rewarded by those same customers recommending the network to others.

Not surprisingly, being pleasant works for small companies too. Drybar, a chain of blowout salons—places where frizzy hair is tamed via blow dryer into styles including the Straight Up (pointy) or the Mai Tai (beach casual)[10]—grew from the backseat of founder Alli Webb's car to more than $70 million in revenue in just seven years.[11] How? By capitalizing on a booming blowout market, yes (there were no blowout salons in the United States in 2007 but today there are hundreds[12]), but also with a focus on "nice," which includes:

- A consistent look: Every salon is decorated in the same yellow and gray color palette, complete with fresh yellow roses.[13]
- A consistent experience: Customers are offered coffee, champagne, or cookies (or all three) and subtitled movies during their appointment.[14]
- A consistent result: Drybar has never expanded its in-salon services and remains focused on one thing: blowouts. "We've been approached by so many different people," said Webb. "We can sell so much, but we choose to be clean, consistent and perfect. You don't always have to listen to what everyone suggests."[15]

Drybar achieves this consistency with a rigorous focus on process, reinforced by a training program (there's an educator in every salon) that covers everything from techniques for creating signature blowout styles to how to chat amiably with clients.[16]

"One of the biggest pillars of our success is customer service," said Webb. "We really think we're like a bar, so when people come in, you have to know their name and things about them that create loyalty. . . . There are times where, you know, we mess up.

It's that customer service of telling them, 'We are sorry. We know we made a mistake. Let us make it up to you.'"[17]

Your Smokey Bear Moment: "Only YOU Can Prevent Customer Rage"

This is serious stuff, and seriously under-used by most businesses. One of the reasons that "process" can seem dry at cocktail parties is that most of the white papers, books, and conferences on Lean, Six Sigma, and others, focus on impossibly large industrial processes such as making semiconductor chips or automobiles, or on massive back-office production operations such as insurance-claims processing or accounts payable automation. These are important projects; they typically save millions of dollars for large companies and often hundreds or thousands of jobs that otherwise might have left communities that depend upon them. Yet they can seem irrelevant to those in non-production parts of a company (six out of the seven customer value-creation processes) or even those who *are* involved in production but at tiny companies (e.g., a job shop that bends or forges metal, or the kitchen at a local restaurant).

Yet these tiny companies, and the functions outside of production, may need process improvement even more. It's simple math: the fewer customers you have, the less you can afford to lose even one of them.

And make no mistake: you are at greater risk than ever before.

Why? Because according to Arizona State University's W. P. Carey School of Business, there's an epidemic of customer rage sweeping the country (and world). In fact, according to the school's most recent survey, 60 percent of US households experienced at least one instance of "customer rage" in the past year. Yet 56 percent of those outraged enough to complain got nothing—nada, zilch, the big goose egg—in return for their terrible service.[18]

Too bad, so sad, right?

Wrong.

Customers who got at least some satisfaction after their complaint told an average of ten to sixteen people about the problem they had. But the ones who got the full Rolling Stones treatment (that is, *no* satisfaction), told twenty-eight people what nincompoopish losers their (likely former) suppliers are.[19]

Small companies simply cannot afford to have twenty-eight other customers or potential customers hear about a massive screw-up, and about the massive wall of silence the wounded customer encountered after requesting restitution, or an apology, or maybe just a sympathetic ear.

As Drybar's Webb said: "If one woman had a bad experience, chances are that probably happened to a bunch of other women and they just didn't tell us."[20]

Yet this happens in business after business, industry after industry. In just one example, some 40 percent of customers who experience problems ordering from a website never order from that company again.[21] This is an enormous problem for online retailers, since many order problems involve delivery and frequently have nothing to do with the retailer itself. Why? Because they deliver to people who may be at work, or are traveling, or who live in apartments or remote areas; in any event, they aren't around when the package arrives. This means that many shipments are lost, or taken in by a forgetful neighbor, or even stolen. This obviously isn't the fault of the retailer, but it creates a terrible experience nonetheless—one that may lose a customer forever. Amazon is managing this issue with process innovation by installing delivery lockers or building storefront locations in major cities in the Unites States and around the world. This allows customers to choose home delivery *or* shipment to a locker or store where the package waits safely for customer retrieval. Other online retailers are either partnering with legacy shipping companies (Deutsche Post DHL offers free lockers for pickup in Germany)[22] or newer technology firms (Estonia-based Cleveron provides shipper-agnostic, smartphone-enabled lockers that allow businesses or consumers to collect or pay, respectively, upon pickup of an item).[23]

And when a process this important gets screwed up, opportunities abound for smaller businesses too. In this instance, they can profit by joining delivery networks like PUDO (Pick Up and Drop Off),[24] an Ontario-based network of more than 1,500 convenience stores and other businesses across Canada[25] that accept and hold package deliveries for local customers. The customer pays three dollars to five dollars per package (depending on weight) for the service, with the store keeping one dollar *and* enjoying increased traffic (and, presumably, additional sales).

Which Improvement Methodology Should *My* Company/Department/Team Use?

The quick and easy answer is: any of them.

The long answer is: It is theoretically possible that one methodology will work significantly better in your industry, or with the personalities on your team, than another. There's no lack of options:

- Lean and its subpractices and variants (*Kaizen, Hoshin Kanri, Poka-yoke*)
- Six Sigma
- Lean Six Sigma
- Total quality management
- Theory of constraints
- Design of experiments
- Reengineering
- Zero-Loss thinking
- Etc., ad infinitum

There's also no lack of consultants who will try to convince you that one methodology is better than all the others, *especially* for you—usually (and not coincidentally) the methodology that the consultant understands and is trying to sell you. (Remember what grandma used to say: "If the only tool you have is a hammer, everything looks like a nail.") Listen politely to the consultants if you must, but take your time before you make a commitment. Talk to peers, meet with competitors at conferences and at their facilities (if you can), study industry literature, and think deeply about which improvement methodology seems to best fit your processes and personalities.

Most of all, though: don't worry about getting it exactly right, because there is no exactly right answer.

Case in point: MPI research among manufacturers finds that there is little difference in the performance of companies using different improvement methodologies (we asked about all the usual suspects such as Lean, Six Sigma, *blah blah blah*). In other words, *it doesn't matter* which methodology you pick.

What *does* matter? Three things:

1. *Having an improvement methodology.* Companies with an improvement methodology significantly outperform those that don't.[26] (Duh.)

2. *Having an improvement methodology for a long time.* Companies with longer periods of implementation of an improvement methodology significantly outperform those with shorter programs. I once heard a webinar participant ask Jim Womack, author of *The Machine That Changed the World* (the book that made Lean famous), how long it takes for a company to *become* Lean. His answer: "Well, Toyota has been at it for sixty years, and they don't think they're done."

3. *Embedding your improvement methodology in every part of the organization.* Companies with more extensive implementations of their improvement methodologies, as measured by number of employees engaged in the initiative, significantly outperform those with less extensive programs.[27]

In short: Pick a program. Stick with it. Get everybody to participate. And for God's sake, get going!

What Business Are You In?

This brings up an important point: when you're working on process, it is imperative to focus on the critical paths that help you to run your business and make money. You must make every process as standardized, repeatable, effective, and high-quality as possible. This is half of how you will make money and satisfy customers.

The other half is how you manage when things go wrong.

Because if experience has taught us anything, it's that Murphy was right: anything that can go wrong, eventually will. How you handle these inevitable screw-ups with customers is crucial to your ongoing relationship with them (as noted in chapter 3 on page **XX**). This means that even as you are improving processes for things to go right in your business, you must also have a process for when things go wrong.

This is harder than it looks, because it's not always easy to anticipate what manner of Nincompoopery or misfortune will be visited upon you. That's why smart companies work hard to anticipate problems and develop guiding principles that allow flexibility so that employees can leverage *Oops!* moments into deeper customer relationships.

A terrific example of this is online shoe retailer Zappos. Stories of the company's customer service are legendary, including:

- the best man whose shoes were lost in transit by UPS, leaving him barefoot for the wedding, until Zappos sent another pair via overnight delivery for free (both the shipping and the shoes);[28] or
- that time a Zappos employee visited a competitor's brick-and-mortar store to find a pair of shoes for a customer staying in Las Vegas, because Zappos had run out of that style;[29] or
- those flowers the company sent to a woman with feet numbed by medical treatment, along with a get-well note;[30] or
- the ten-hour, twenty-nine-minute phone call with a customer who just wanted to talk, a lot, before buying a pair of UGG boots.[31]

The list goes on and on. And so does Zappos's customer loyalty: roughly three-quarters of all Zappos orders are from existing customers, which makes a focus on the process of customer service and on fixing screw-ups a vastly better investment than marketing or advertising. Explained Zappos CEO Tony Hsieh: "Our whole philosophy became 'Let's take most of the money we would've spent on advertising and paid marketing and instead of spending it on that, invest it in the customer experience/customer service, and then let our customers do the marketing for us through word of mouth,' and that became the whole business model."[32]

Oops! Moments Are Even Easier to Fix If You're a Small Company

Only a lunatic would tell you to start screwing up just to build customer relationships. But leaders at small companies and start-ups should remember that they are better positioned than large companies to take advantage of creative, make-good customer service. Why? Because small companies are (duh) small, and vastly nimbler, and typically far closer to their customers than larger competitors. All you need is a process to track *when* service goes off the rails and for *what* you'll do about it.

A great example of this is Zocdoc, a start-up that smooths the anxiety-laden process of finding a new doctor and scheduling an appointment via online software. Founded in 2007, the company has developed an enviable reputation for customer service; when patients experienced service issues during Zocdoc's formative years, Dr. Oliver Kharraz, a founder and current COO, would personally meet customers at their physicians' offices to apologize.[33]

"People were definitely surprised that after using a free service on the Internet, which they kind of expected not to work perfectly anyway, they find a guy with flowers and chocolate waiting for them," explained Kharraz. "Obviously that wasn't scalable, but we wanted in every instance to understand if something didn't work out, what was the root cause? We need to make it right for the individual and all of those coming after her to make sure the problem gets eradicated."[34]

As Zocdoc grew, the company worked hard to standardize customer service practices that build long-term relationships and collect customer intelligence that improves processes at Zocdoc itself, via technology, metrics, and culture:

- *Technology*: The firm's check-in service lets patients complete medical forms before an office visit; an automated text is sent to the patient at the time of his or her appointment, requesting confirmation that everything is okay with the documents. If a patient reports a problem, he or she receives an immediate phone call from a customer service representative to assist.

- *Metrics*: Like any organization seeking to improve processes, Zocdoc puts effort into determining which metrics to track—in this case, the percentage of emails that receive a response within one hour, and the percentage of calls answered after a single ring. These numbers are displayed on a monitor in the customer service department for all employees to see, along with a constant stream of tweets coming in about Zocdoc.

- *Culture*: Most important of all, the company's customer service representatives have authority to do whatever it takes to assist patients, whether by staying on the phone to help with an internet search or by locating family members late to appointments. Said Anna Ellwood, director of operations: "If there is any industry where service should be paramount, it should be healthcare."[35]

Talent and Process Reinforce Each Other

One of the things emphasized by companies that excel in process is the importance of talent in executing those processes. In other words, is there a culture of process excellence here? This is a critical insight; at Zappos, for example, it wasn't just a rigorous focus on process that made the company a service legend. The retailer invests heavily in making sure that employees understand, embrace, and execute established processes in ways that create great experiences for customers.

- The company has located both its headquarters and call center in the same city (Las Vegas, Nevada), to make sure everyone stays in sync on the importance of customer loyalty.
- All new hires at Zappos, regardless of role or salary, work for a month as customer service representatives and then spend a week in the company's Kentucky logistics facility, before assuming their actual positions.[36]
- During each employee's initial training period, he or she is offered $4,000 to quit. Why? Because the last thing

you want in a customer service employee is someone who doesn't want to be there. For only $4,000, Zappos kindly and efficiently allows uncommitted associates to eliminate themselves from the employee pool before they poison customer or colleague relationships (about 2–3 percent of new hires accept the departure offer). Even better, those who refuse the offer have made an active choice to stay and to embrace Zappos's culture.[37]

This focus on culture has resulted in employee loyalty rivaling that of Zappos's customers. When the company relocated its call center from California to Las Vegas in 2005, 80 percent of its thirteen-dollar-per-hour employees moved as well. Zappos's employee retention rate (85 percent) is also dramatically higher than the industry average.[38]

"We've made company culture our No. 1 priority and have formed our entire company strategy around that," said Hsieh. "Culture drives brand, customer service and [ultimately] growth."[39]

Zappos Core Values[40]

1. Deliver WOW through customer service
2. Embrace and drive change
3. Create fun and a little weirdness
4. Be adventurous, creative, and open-minded
5. Pursue growth and learning
6. Build open and honest relationships with communication
7. Build a positive team and family spirit

8. Do more with less
9. Be passionate and determined
10. Be humble

Process culture is equally important at small firms such as Zingerman's, a Michigan delicatessen that's grown into what *Inc.* magazine called "The Coolest Small Company in America." Founded in 1985, the restaurant expanded from selling memorable sandwiches—"So big you needed two hands to hold them and the dressing would roll down your forearms," according to cofounder Paul Saginaw—into Ann Arbor's Zingerman Community of Businesses (ZCoB), incorporating a bakery, creamery, other restaurants, and catering and retail operations, among others.[41]

Yet the engine that drives consistent, profitable growth across ZCoB is an intense focus on process, embodied in the education provided to employees (and outside customers) by ZingTrain (part of ZCoB). ZingTrain maps value-creation processes within ZCoB's businesses (e.g., 5 Steps to Handling Customer Complaints, 3 Steps to Great Finance) and then uses them as discussion topics in internal and external seminars.[42]

An added benefit of training employees on process, explained ZingTrain managing partner Maggie Bayless, is how processes themselves can be improved through documentation and teaching. "When we founded ZingTrain," she said, "We were forced to get more systematic about clearly defining our values, operating principles, and specific learning objectives. We started creating frameworks for 'recipes' teaching the key principles of the business. . . . We're a food business, so everyone is used to the concept of recipes. [But] what we do is create recipes not only for good food, but also for customer service, finance, visioning, and

111

other practices that are central to the organization. For instance, from the beginning, customer service was very important at Zingerman's—so much so that we track it as one of our three bottom lines, along with food quality and financial health. Even before ZingTrain, we had developed a recipe for *3 Steps to Great Service*, which we taught to all employees. It became a time-tested approach and the template for much of our training work."[43]

Zingerman's Three Steps to Great Service[44]

1. Figure out what the customer wants.
2. Get it for them—accurately, politely, enthusiastically.
3. Go the extra mile.

Talent and Process Reinforce Innovation

But wait: the real fun and the real money start when you combine all three: talent, process, and innovation. A great example of this is Vermeer Corporation, a manufacturer of agricultural, utility, recycling, and forestry equipment. The company started its improvement journey by focusing on Lean, in part by conducting Kaizen events. A Kaizen event is a focused improvement effort in a short period of time (a half-day, several days) in which managers and employees in a department or production line fix as many problems as they can, eliminating waste and becoming more efficient.[45]

Standard process stuff, so far.

Here's where it gets interesting. As Vermeer's customers heard about the successful Kaizen events, opportunities arose for Vermeer to assist customers in *their* improvement efforts. In short order, Vermeer began replicating what Procter & Gamble did with its Downy fabric softener in Mexico (page **XX** in chapter 2); they began observing select customers on job sites while they used Vermeer equipment, so that Vermeer employees could offer suggestions for process improvements. At the end of these visits, some lasting a week, Vermeer employees made recommendations on how customers can improve productivity.[46]

"We watch how they are using the equipment," said Vermeer chairman Mary Andringa, "How much time they are spending looking for things, whether they are having difficulty with a certain process in the construction, or a problem with the equipment itself. Then we question what we can do to take some waste points out of their process."[47]

Not surprisingly, customers love this, because they learn to be more efficient and make more money at no additional cost. It creates tremendous goodwill, but there's a far more important outcome for Vermeer. It gives employees detailed feedback on how the company's equipment is used in the field, and what aspects of design or reliability might be improved. Explained Andringa: "We talk to customers not only about product design but factors most crucial to them, and how we can address them. For instance, equipment reliability is a huge concern, as is commonality of platform and parts. Given their difficulty in finding skilled workers, customers don't want to have to retrain people on different models of equipment. We have to make the equipment simple and reliable. . . . This requires not just talking to customers, but visiting job sites and talking to operators."[48]

Vermeer hit the trifecta with this program: they used their own process and talent to help customers with their innovation, in turn driving more innovation at Vermeer.

Twenty-First-Century Process Improvement (You Can Do This Too)

One of the most encouraging business developments of the (relatively) new century is the democratization of process opportunities with customers—specifically, the availability of new techniques and new technologies to improve processes at businesses large and small. We're not talking about Lean, or enterprise resource planning (ERP) software, or analytics; we're talking about social media. Why? Because at its root, process is about communication: sharing information, collaboration, and problem-solving skills and ideas. Social media provides an affordable platform for any company to include customers in process improvements and problem-solving.

A great example is airline JetBlue, a long-time user of Twitter to communicate with customers in transit, with dedicated staff monitoring the company's feed. In one instance, travel blogger Dave Raffaele tweeted:

> *@jetblue*: You need to turn down the heat on your 7:55 p.m.
> flight from Boston to Denver. It was rough.

Less than two minutes later, JetBlue responded, also via Twitter:

JetBlue: thanks for the heads up! (Sometimes flight crews get overzealous traveling from cold to cold!)

But Raffaele wasn't through with suggestions for better customer service:

@jetblue: In Denver and want to check my bag but there is no one at the counter. What's wrong with this picture?

Another Twitter user beat JetBlue to the punch, but not by much:

JetBlue: @sogrady is a step ahead of me—but sending a note to the GM and Supes as a heads-up anyway. Are there many waiting?

More Twitter conversation ensued between Raffaele and JetBlue, concluding with this reassuring tweet:

JetBlue: You should see some Crewmembers showing up shortly—our offices in DEN are away from the ticket counter.

JetBlue's costs for leveraging social media are low, but the investment delivers high value to individual customers, even as it generates a halo effect of goodwill among the rest of the company's Twitter followers. In a sense, the company asks for customers to help it improve processes and outcomes in real time, highlighting JetBlue's responsiveness to everyone on Twitter.[49]

Yes, This Works for Small Companies Too

Okay, good for JetBlue, but you're not running a $6 billion business with 20,000 employees[50] and a social media team. Can this work for you?

That depends: How creative are you willing to be? Pittsburgh's Franktuary, an upscale hot dog joint (tagline: *Franks, Poutine, Libations*), keeps customers happy across three locations by engaging them on multiple platforms:[51]

Facebook (Franktuary Lawrenceville)

It's always a special moment when a party orders The Last Supper. 12 franks, 8 toppings. Never fails to impress both our staff and our guests. If you have a reason to celebrate, keep this bad-boy in mind.

> **Taracat Cayce Loversidge:** do you make a vegetarian version??
>
> **Franktuary Lawrenceville:** Taracat Cayce Loversidge yes!
>
> **Taracat Cayce Loversidge:** I CANT WAIT, SEE YOU IN FEBRUARY!!
>
> **Casey Baker:** I want this in place of a wedding cake[52]

Twitter (@ Franktuary)

We were proud to contribute to the incredible @strawforward campaign via Sustainable Pittsburgh (@dine_sustainpgh)

Check out the wild art that was made from all the used straws that were collected![53]

Instagram (franktuary)

Want to join our kitchen team? The Franktuary is looking for responsible, hardworking, clean, and friendly people to work in our kitchen in Lawrenceville. [54]

And remember: this is for *hot dogs*. You can definitely do this in your business.

What Are You Waiting For?

When your customers really need you—when something goes wrong, when it's after hours—how can they find you?

More importantly, how are you going to deliver a great process innovation this year? What will your customers say about how you're improving processes for their customer value, not just this year but next year too, and the year after that?

Anti-Nincompoopery Planning: Process

Remember *This*.	Then Ask Yourself *This*!
Look at your company through your customer's eyes.	**Research and Development:** How do we imagine, innovate, and design great new products and services that customers can't wait to buy? **Procurement:** How do we find and source all the materials, components, supplies, talent, and technology required to create great products and services? **Administration:** How do we manage all the boring but incredibly important back-office stuff that allows for the creation of great products and services (i.e. finance, human resources, maintenance, etc.)? **Logistics:** How do we coordinate shipments of all the stuff we procure to the right places (our offices, stores, plants, etc.), and then deliver great products and services to customers, with as little stress as possible? **Sales and Marketing:** How do we make customers aware that we have great products and services, and then facilitate purchases in ways that create new value for customers? **Production and Performance:** How do we build great products and services with quality and speed? **Service and Support:** How do we stay with customers after the sale to make sure that great products and services do what they're supposed to do, and make our customers' businesses more profitable or their lives better?

Big Process Job #1 *Fix or kill.*	At which of the functions above are we terrible? Can we change the process? Can we change (improve or remove) the people managing the process? Can we get rid of the process altogether, by finding someone else to do it for us (outsourcing)? Can we quit the process altogether by exiting that product or service or process?
Big Process Job #2 *Improve.*	At which of the functions above are we okay or only sort-of-okay? How can we improve the process, or least stop irritating our customers quite as much?
Big Process Job #3 *Excel.*	At which of the functions above are we great? How did we get great at this process in the first place? How can we become even greater?
Measure, measure, measure!	Do we have effective internal measures of our key process steps? How can we get them? Are effective external comparison measures of our key process steps available? How can we get them? If we can't get effective external comparison measures of our key process steps, can we SWAG (Scientific Wild-Ass Guess) at them?
Validate, validate, validate.	Do our customers really value the process we're about to improve?
Only *you* can prevent customer rage.	How will we handle inevitable screw-ups with customers? What is our process for when things go wrong? How can we leverage new technologies to help mitigate customer frustrations, and create customer delight?

CHAPTER 5

Getting Started:

Obstacles and Opportunities

If Avoiding Nincompoopery Is So Simple, Why Isn't Everybody Doing It?

Let us begin with a philosophical inquiry into the existential nature of Nincompoopery. If, based on experience, we can assert the following.

a. Nincompoopery not only exists, but abounds, in our organizations and those of our competitors.
b. Therefore, if we can simply avoid or minimize Nincompoopery ourselves, we should be able to outwit our (still-nincompoopish) competitors and enjoy increasing market share and profits.

And yet we don't.
Why?

It could be that we ourselves are incurable nincompoops; one of the hallmarks of being a nincompoop is the inability to recognize that you are a nincompoop. In fact, many nincompoops live long, self-satisfied lives, blissfully unaware of the havoc they leave in their wakes.

Let's assume we're not among them.

If so, then the good news is that we are not nincompoops, and therefore have incredible opportunities to reinvent the customer value that our companies create, improving our customers' lives and our bottom lines.

The bad news is that even with this incredible advantage of not being nincompoops, most of us still won't change our companies or improve our own lives.

Again, why?

You Can Always Find Somebody to Tell You You're Wrong

Mostly, it's because we listen to the wrong people. It's easy to do, because there are so many of them, in so many different flavors of dysfunction, indifference, and despair, especially in the workplace. In fact, it's often hard to keep up with all the many reasons these naysayers cite for why-you-will-obviously-fail. But they, and their poison utterances, really fall into just three categories.

1. *Woe is all of us.* Nothing will ever change, all our customers/managers/employees/etc. are denser than neutron stars, and you are just wasting your time.
2. *Woe is you.* You don't know enough, you've only been [in

this industry/an employee here/a manager/alive/etc.] for [a
year/five years/twenty years/forever/etc.].

3. *Woe is change.* Okay, *maybe* that could work, and maybe
I could even like that change, but . . . that would be hard.
How could you/we ever do that?

Those in group 1 (*Woe is all of us*) are nincompoops who
have given up. And make no mistake, there are lots of them.
A study from Gallup, Inc. found that 85 percent of employees
aren't "engaged" at work, a statistic that seems unsurprising to
anyone who's ever visited a Department of Motor Vehicles office
or tried to get cable installed.[1] Be polite to these folks (why create unnecessary enemies?), but avoid them at all costs; although
mostly harmless (they don't care enough to cause mischief), their
negativity will suck your soul out through your nostrils. If you
can't avoid their presence, step over them as gingerly as you can.
There is no future for them or you in Woe-Is-Us Land.

Those in group 2 (*Woe is you*) are also nincompoops, but
far more dangerous. They will sap your confidence in one of
two ways.

- *Intentionally*: They'll listen to your ideas with a semi-polite
half-smirk and then offer some version of: "Why would
anybody listen to you?" This is poison. Although you'll be
tempted to argue (flinging some version of "Because it's
a good idea, you ninny!" back at them), it's futile; these
people have given up every bit as much as those in group 1,
but have also gone a step backward on the evolution scale.
These Woe-Is-You-ers believe that because they can't be successful, then no one else could (or should) succeed either, lest

they be reminded of what tiny, whiny nitwits they are. In essence, they've weaponized their own self-loathing against anyone who seeks change or improvement in a desperate attempt to make sure that everyone else loathes themselves too. Why? Because consciously or unconsciously, they need to reassure themselves that their lack of effort in changing their miserable states is not their faults, but just the predictable, inevitable order of things. *Run* from these people, step around them if you must, or (if neither of those options is available) crush them like bugs (metaphorically and office-politics-wise, of course). You cannot, will not, succeed with these confidence saboteurs around you.

- *Unintentionally*: Fortunately, the vast majority of those in group 2 aren't actively evil, but will undermine your self-confidence nonetheless. These are the coworkers who say: "Well, that sounds like a good idea, but maybe we should [insert one: check with the boss/do some more research/ set up another meeting/form a committee/etc.]." These are nice people—they don't mean to harm you or impede your efforts to innovate—but their lack of self-confidence and fear of the future is every bit as profound as those who would intentionally harm you. The only difference between these two groups is that the Unintentionals undermine change not by sabotage but through worry, fear, delay, and endless rehashing of previous decisions and programs that didn't work out as planned. You probably can't avoid these people at work (there are lots and lots of them), but you can limit the amount of time that you spend with Unintentionals, and the amount of their negativity that you absorb. The good news is that as soon as you start to make progress, these folks will come along (although more slowly than you would like). Be patient, and know that they will be with you eventually, and might even shed their nincompoop ways (change is possible for people as well as organizations).

All of which brings us to group 3 (*Woe is change*). These people might sometimes act nincompoopishly, but mostly they're hoping that you, or somebody like you, will show them how things can be different and better (i.e., free of Nincompoopery). Listen to their fears, assuage their anxieties, but above all embrace them. These people will, with the right leadership, coaching, and encouragement from you, reinvent customer value for your customers, the culture of your firm, and your bottom line.

Plus, you'll all have a lot more fun.

Ready, Set . . . Wait!

So now you're ready to go. You're ignoring the hopeless, inspiring the hopeful, and ready to lead the (cautiously) committed. All you need to get started is . . . What?

A strategy and a plan, for sure. You can't reinvent innovation, talent, and process without first creating a road map from where you, your team, and your organization are now, to where you need to go.

But a road map is only half of the battle.

The other, harder half is making sure that everyone on your team will *follow* a road map. This means that you'll have to develop a second strategy to motivate your team to want to change, and (even more important) for you to manage and neu-tralize resistance to change.

It would be lovely, of course, if there were no resistance to the change that you hope to lead. And if, in some magical cir-cumstance, your idea is so great, and the need for it is so clear, that everyone in the conference room falls to their knees and raises their arms and sings hosannas about your brainstorm—well, that will pretty much be the best day at work you'll ever have. Congrats to you, and please share some of your managerial pixie dust with the rest of us.

In the real world, of course, change is not easy, and resistance is not only common, but to be expected. Why? Because while everyone says that they want change, they usually only like it if it means that nothing will be different, and if they don't have to work very hard at it.

Alas, this is not how change works.

Resistance to Change Is Normal, and Often Healthy

Resistance is a basic human response to the uncertainty that accompanies any change, even one with potentially good out-comes. Psychology studies have proven that uncertainty creates significant discomfort for most of us, and extreme duress for some. In one experiment, subjects were told that they could receive a harsher electrical jolt now ("like a strong insect bite") or a milder shock later ("a strong buzz"). A full 70 percent opted for more pain now, simply to avoid the uncertainty of waiting.[2] In other words, most people would rather continue with the pain and dysfunction that they're familiar with rather than endure the uncertainty, dread, and discomfort that comes with waiting to see what change might bring.

Is it any wonder, then, that it's hard to motivate people to change, even if they understand that it will benefit not just customers, or the company, but themselves too?

Fortunately, there are ways to minimize and ameliorate the pain of uncertainty around change. "The key to the problem is to understand the true nature of resistance," wrote Paul Lawrence, a sociologist and professor at the Harvard Business School. "Actually, what employees resist is usually not technical change but social change—the change in their human relationships that generally accompanies technical change."[3]

This is critical to remember: the resistance that you encounter in leading change is not usually or mostly about the change itself but about *anxiety*. More specifically, resistance is the public expression of the private worries, insecurities, and fears that your bosses and coworkers have about the impact of change on:

- their continued employment (*If this crazy change goes through, will I still have a job?*),
- their daily tasks (*Will my life at work be better or worse than it is now?*),
- their status (both official and unofficial) within the organization (*Will my title change? Will my opinion still matter? Will people still respect me at work, in the industry, in my community, and at home?*), and
- their self-esteem (*Will I feel better or worse about my work and about myself?*).

Unfortunately, your bosses and colleagues won't publicly articulate these fears, and, in fact, may not even be aware of them (not everyone is introspective or self-aware). But these feelings are so common, and so human, that you must expect them. It's similar to what happens when you disagree or argue with a friend, family member, or spouse: often the source of conflict is not the proximate event (for example, you didn't load the dishwasher properly, or you forgot to send your nephew a wedding gift), but instead an unspoken concern that your lack of empathy means that you simply don't care enough about the other person's feelings. At home or at a family reunion, how you choose to address the underlying concern will determine the quality and strength of your relationship with the other person going forward. At work the stakes are even higher: how you choose to manage the anxieties of your peers, or how you ignore them, will determine whether you can be successful in leading change or not.

It's important to remember, too, that because resistance is born of anxiety, which resides inside the worried heads and hearts of the resisters, it is emphatically *not* defiance of you, or a lack of respect for you or your ideas. It is fear of change, pure and simple. This makes it imperative that you not personalize resistance, but think of it instead as a gift—one that gives you a chance to explain the need for change, influence the right people to help you, and persuade everyone else to try something new. If you're empathetic enough to recognize resistance as a cry for help, and kind (and strategic) enough to use it for good, everyone wins. "When resistance *does* appear," Lawrence continued, "it should not be thought of as something to be *overcome*. Instead, it can best be thought of as a useful red flag—a signal that something is going wrong. To use a rough analogy, signs of resistance in a social organization are useful in the same way that pain is useful to the body as a signal that some bodily functions are getting out of adjustment."[4]

This leads to an enduring leadership truth: as smart as you are, as right as you are, and as urgently needed as your change initiative is, *you cannot force your team to change.* You can create the conditions for change to be possible. You can create incentives that make people more likely to choose change. You can marginalize, isolate, or fire irredeemable lunkheads who actively sabotage change. But the decision to change—or not—rests solely with each individual on your team or in your company.

You're a Leader Now, and That Means You're a Politician

So how do you create the conditions for success and change?

Politics.

Politics (whether in Washington, DC, or any capital, or in your corporate headquarters or local store, plant, or office) is widely despised today, with some reason. The litany of do-nothing-ism, backstabbing, corruption, and self-dealing that can be attributed to evildoers in legislative back rooms or at our own companies is too long to list. In fact, while 76 percent of workers say office politics are necessary to get ahead, the top tactics recognized by political players and their victims alike are a dismal lot:

- Gossiping or spreading rumors (46 percent)
- Gaining favor by flattering the boss (28 percent)
- Taking credit for others' work (17 percent)

- Sabotaging coworkers' projects (5 percent)[5]

Yuck. And yet politics is not really any of the above. All those are just terrible tactics and behaviors, often on display near public budgets, corporate treasuries, or the office donut box. In short, they're all bad politics, or criminal behavior. Yet this skullduggery is a vanishingly small part of what really happens in politics of any kind. The vast majority of politicians, whether in government or corporations, perform dutiful service by practicing good politics to get good things done—in other words, *change*.

What are good politics? For that answer, that let's return to our dictionary. There are many nuances for the word *politics*, but for our purposes these three from *Merriam-Webster* serve best:

3a: political affairs or business; especially: competition
between competing interest groups or individuals
for power and leadership (as in a government)

[and]

5a: the total complex of relations between
people living in society

[but most usefully]

5b: relations or conduct in a particular area of
experience especially as seen or dealt with from
a political point of view <*office* politics>[6]

Please note: by definition, politics is not inherently dirty, corrupting, or evil, regardless of its setting. It is, simply, the art of getting things done with other people.

Good Politicians Get Good Things Done

Don't kid yourself: to lead, you need to play. "The biggest political mistake [most leaders make] is to assume that organizational politics doesn't exist," said John Eldred, president of Transition One Associates, an organizational dynamics consulting firm, and cofounder of the Wharton School Family Business Program. "It's often a question of language. When we win on an issue, we call it leadership. When we lose, we call it politics. Practicing politics simply means increasing your options for effective results."[7]

Marie McIntyre, author of *Secrets to Winning at Office Politics*, offered the golden rule for good workplace politics: "You should never advance your own interests by hurting the business or harming other people."[8]

Lovely words. But not nearly as easy as it sounds.

In every friendship, relationship, family, or organization, we're all stuck in what German philosopher Arthur Schopenhauer described as the Porcupine's Dilemma:

> On a cold winter's day a community of porcupines huddled very close together to protect themselves from freezing through their mutual warmth. However, they soon felt one another's quills, which then forced them apart. Now when the need for warmth brought them closer together again, that second drawback repeated itself so that they were tossed back and forth between both kinds of suffering until they discovered

a moderate distance from one another, at which they could best endure the situation.—This is how the need for society, arising from the emptiness and monotony of our own inner selves, drives people together; but their numerous repulsive qualities and unbearable flaws push them apart once again. The middle distance they finally discover and at which a coexistence is possible is courtesy and good manners. In England, anyone who does not stay at this distance is told: 'Keep your distance!'—Of course by means of this the need for mutual warmth is only partially satisfied, but in exchange the prick of the quills is not felt.—Yet whoever has a lot of his own inner warmth prefers to stay away from society in order neither to cause trouble nor to receive it.[9]

For our purposes, this means that it's really hard to get sharp-edged porcupines, or humans, to work together (on change or improving customer value), because it's much safer for each of us to keep our distance (by doing things the way we always have, even if it doesn't really work, because at least we won't get pricked and be worse off). Our competing interests—desire for change, desire for security, desire for certainty, desire for respect, desire for an improved bottom line—often paralyze our efforts to work together.

This is where good politics comes in. We know from our definition that politics is how competing interests are managed peacefully and effectively, whether those of groups or individuals. This means that you cannot lead change, or persuade others to choose change (i.e., be a good politician) without understanding the competing interests of your team or stakeholders.

But how can you find out what those competing interests are?

You could ask, of course, but that's unlikely to be effective. As noted earlier, many people are not self-aware enough to understand their own motivations, and others may be reluctant to share them—especially those motivations having to do with fear or anxiety—to avoid appearing weak or self-serving. In fact, if you press too hard in asking people to reveal their deepest fears or emotions, or to be "open" about what they want and need, you may encourage less communication and increase the resistance to change that you're trying to reduce.

Fortunately, however, there are models of organizational behavior that allow us to make good guesses as to what some of these competing interests will be. (See "What Do These Prickly Porcupines Want from You?" sidebar.)

What Do These Prickly Porcupines Want from You?

It depends whom you ask. Psychologists, sociologists, anthropologists, and organizational behavior analysts have tried for more than a century to describe what it is that humans want, and by extension, what it is that bosses, colleagues, and employees want. A sampling of useful models might include:

- Psychologist Abraham Maslow postulated his hierarchy of needs in 1943, and despite later criticism, his ideas still influence our understanding of human motivation. Often depicted as a pyramid (more basic needs on the bottom, more abstract needs toward the top), Maslow's hierarchy posits that humans have five categories of need, and that each need must, in general (but not always), be satisfied before the next, higher-level need can be considered. These are:

- *Physiological* (air, food, water, sex, etc.)
- *Safety* (physical security, income, property, health, etc.)
- *Social* (family, friends, intimacy, etc.)
- *Ego* (self-esteem, respect, confidence, achievement, etc.)
- *Self-actualizing* (morality, creativity, problem-solving, personal growth, etc.)[10]

- Psychologist Robert Hogan asserted that there are three "master motives" for human beings in the workplace:
  - *Get along*: Are these are my people? Do I belong here? Do they like me?
  - *Get ahead*: Where do I rank in this group? How can I move higher?
  - *Find meaning*: How does this group help me find a way to make sense of the world, and my life in it?[11]

- In *Driven: How Human Nature Shapes Our Choices*, Paul Lawrence and Nitin Nohria identified our basic human drives as:

  - *Acquire*: How can I get and maintain wealth, knowledge, and respect?
  - *Bond*: How can I build meaningful relationships with others, based on reciprocity?
  - *Learn*: How can I understand the world, and my place in it?
  - *Defend*: How can I protect what matters to me— wealth, family, values, etc.?[12]

A cynic might look at these behavioral rubrics in the context of ten thousand years of (often bad) human behavior and conclude: no matter how much you dress us up, no matter how many beautiful paintings we scratch onto our cave walls, we're still a bunch of Neanderthals trying to figure out how to stand on the tallest rock without getting knocked off by somebody else's club.

But someone a bit more hopeful—you, perhaps—might look at these and see three Big Requirements for Change.

Big Requirement for Change #1: Security.

First and foremost, people need to feel safe. They need to know that their incomes and their persons are secure, and that change won't increase their level of worry or insecurity in the long run. It's helpful, too, if you can truthfully outline how, in a best-case scenario, change could actually increase their security and comfort.

Big Requirement for Change #2: Relationships.

People need to know that their feelings, relationships, and social status will be considered during change, even if they can't be fully preserved or protected in their current states. Given a chance, people are generally reasonable and understand that during change, their roles and relative statuses may evolve; this is uncomfortable, but can be accepted if they know that they will be respected.

Big Requirement for Change #3: Meaning.

Those ten thousand years of human experience also reveal that once we know that we'll survive, and that our relationships with others are secure, we almost always turn our attention to meaning: *What is my life about?* In asking this question, most of us seek to find how our lonely existences connect to something larger, something that imbues our lives with purpose beyond daily struggles for security and social respect. For most people, that *primary* meaning can be found in some combination of faith, values, family, and community. But a *secondary* longing for meaning relates to the reality of our schedules; given that most of us will spend roughly a third of our waking hours at work for roughly half a century (a total of ninety thousand hours or more), we naturally hope that our work will engage us, support our longing for meaning, and serve a purpose deeper than merely providing security for us and our family. We want those ninety thousand hours to mean something more than just time served.

The Good Politician Begins with the End in Mind

Stephen Covey's famous admonition for getting things done— "Begin with the end in mind"[13]—applies to leading change as well, but with a twist: even though the foundational needs of those you lead are security (first) and social relationships (second), you cannot address those two needs first. Why? Because in your company's current state of Nincompoopery, these needs are already being met in one way or another. They may be met poorly or incompletely, but most employees or colleagues or bosses have likely made some sort of disagreeable peace with the company's current nincompoopish situation, at least for now (otherwise, they'd quit). Unless you start with *meaning*, the need or hope for change, you'll just seem nosy and ill-mannered as you ask people over lunch about their worries, their jobs, their inner work lives, and/or their organizational social statuses.

Don't do that. Instead, meet your team's primal needs—the three Big Requirements for Change—in *reverse* order:

Managing Big Requirement for Change #3: Meaning.

To start with the end in mind, bring your team together and outline a compelling need for change and an equally compelling vision of what the future will look like. This will be easier if there's a looming crisis or burning platform (e.g., the company is going bankrupt, or the business unit might close if performance doesn't improve, or a new technology has disrupted the market), because you can simply point to the crisis and say, in effect, "If we don't change, we're going to die (economically)." Fortunately or unfortunately, however, this is rarely the case, which means that you will have to do your homework on what the change will be, what it will require, and what the future state will look like. The more detail you can offer, the more readily your team will accept the need for change. Let's call this the opening speech of the Good Politician's campaign for change (even if the speech is just a PowerPoint or a memo shared at a weekly staff meeting). Announce why change is needed; put forth a plan for how to accomplish it; paint a picture of how much better life will be after the change has been completed; and reiterate the values and principles by which you will live as change happens (such as transparency, inclusiveness, commitment to principles), and thank everyone for joining this journey.

Managing Big Requirement for Change #2: Relationships.

The next phase is critical, because no matter how brilliant the vision is, you've also introduced uncertainty into the lives of your team. The Good Politician understands this, and works with team members one-on-one or in small groups to discuss how to implement the change and to persuade the reluctant to at least *try* the change. This is important operationally, because there is no way for you to effect change for a team without including team members (remember Federal Warehouse in chapter 3). But it is even more critical emotionally and socially. Even positive change will alter the social statuses and lives of your team members; if you can demonstrate your empathy by paying attention to these factors and showing that you understand that change may be uncomfortable or difficult, you will create an environment in which employees can speak up—and feel heard and respected. These people will consequently be more generous with their time, intelligence, and commitment, so *don't skip this phase.* "Empathy involves . . . *feelings*, spoken or unspoken. All of us want to feel respected, and none of us wants to feel stupid, no matter what the situation. When we ignore . . . feelings, we risk causing a bad reaction *no matter how well we take care of the transaction itself.*"[14]

Managing Big Requirement for Change #1: Security.

Although you will need to mention security during the *Meaning* phase (something along the lines of, "We need to do this so that we can guarantee the economic security of our company and our jobs, growing income for everyone"), the uncertain nature of change means that you will not be able to give everyone the answer they want *now*, which is how this will change their job in the *future*. Be direct: "We don't know exactly how this will affect everyone's jobs, but we do know that this change is necessary/unavoidable if we want to survive and thrive. I believe that within X weeks/months we will know precisely how this will shake out." Be clear, concise, and transparent. This will not satisfy everyone, but the one thing that is never forgiven during change is not loss of status, or even the loss of jobs, but the loss of trust because you lied. Be positive, tell the truth, and move expeditiously.

Aetna's near-death experience is a tremendous example of this. In the early 2000s, the company had been through four CEOs in five years, was losing almost $1 million a day, and had many customers (patients, physicians, and health care institutions alike) who hated the company. Why? Because the company's stodgy "Mother Aetna" culture of rule-following underperformance (paraphrased by management guru Jon Katzenbach as, "We take care of our people for life, as long as they show up every day and don't cause trouble") expressed itself in a narrow-minded focus on managing medical costs (minimizing claim payments) at the expense of customer service and relationships. This meant that even as the company succeeded in controlling costs, it succeeded even more grandly in damaging its ability to attract and retain customers. (Hint: This is how you lose $1 million a day.)[15]

This was not an easy fix. Mother Aetna was 150 years old and not inclined to change. Fortunately for her and Aetna's employees, the fourth CEO, John Rowe, took a different approach than his drive-by predecessors. Instead of directing wholesale changes in business processes and culture from the top, he explored Aetna's current culture from the bottom up, to see what, if anything, could be salvaged and repurposed for the future. Via talks and meetings, both formal and informal, with employees at all levels, Rowe interviewed Mother Aetna to see if she had any good qualities left.[16]

Not surprisingly, she did: the Aetna culture reflected decades of pride and concern for patients and health care providers—positive traits that were sometimes forgotten during the company's struggle to adapt to exploding medical costs and an era of managed care.[17]

After this period of discovery, Rowe invested time in all three Big Requirements for Change.

- He announced the arrival of the "New Aetna," a company that would restore pride by refocusing efforts on serving patients and providers, and reestablishing itself as a leading health insurer (*meaning*).
- He looked for ways to connect with employees both personally and in discussions of shared values via meetings, forums, and social activities (*relationships*).
- He spoke plainly about the cost of change. Reinventing Aetna would require a wholesale restructuring and the elimination of five thousand or more jobs, meaning that no job was safe (*security*).[18]

Let's be clear: culture change alone can't fix a failing business, because the underlying structural problems must be addressed as well. At Aetna, a haphazard collection of information technologies often led to duplicate payments, and claims data was so incomplete that the company underpriced premiums and missed financial targets for years. A $20 million information technology overhaul to create an "Executive Management Information

System" gave executives new visibility into Aetna's data, spurring them to raise premiums and cancel unprofitable accounts (actions which did not immediately help Aetna's customer-relationship issues). Aetna also maintained its cost-control focus, but with a new emphasis on comanaging high-cost claims with physicians and patients (for example, a hemophiliac's $500,000-per-month care was reduced by 75 percent, with improved outcomes). During the transformation, Aetna lost eight million of its twenty-one million health care plan members, falling from number one to number three in the market.[19]

And yet, as employees embraced painful changes (and as layoffs abated), internal surveys and conversations reported renewed pride and energy. Gradually a company left for dead by investors came back to life; by the mid-2000s, Aetna was making nearly $5 million a day, flipping a $300 million annual loss into a $1.7 billion profit. The company's stock rose from $5.84 per share (split-adjusted) in 2001 to $48.40 in 2006.[20]

For small companies, a rigorous focus on managing the three core principles of culture (meaning, relationships, security) during change may be even more important. Polly's Coffee, a successful Long Beach, California-based retailer of craft-roasted coffees, nearly died in the late 1990s as two Starbucks opened nearby (one within seventy-eight yards). Despite a twenty-year head start, Polly's saw sales plummet by 10 to 15 percent almost overnight. Newspapers decried the bullying tactics of mega-chains on Main Street America, but nobody had much hope that Polly's could withstand the onslaught.[21]

Owner Michael Sheldrake, along with retail consultant Bob Phibbs, decided to fight back:

- First, they refocused Polly's on what it did best: being intensely local while offering world-class coffee and service (*meaning*). A founding member of the Specialty Coffee Association, Sheldrake roasted Polly's coffee on-site in a wide array of flavors, offering a variety of fresh options unavailable from a chain like Starbucks. He emphasized the local difference with a new crowdsourced logo; sharpened advertising ("Coffee down the street from ordinary"); ran special events (Coffee 101: Brewing the Perfect Cup and Coffee 102: Brewing the Perfect Espresso); and reinvented the in-store experience (new outdoor furniture, upgraded merchandise, repainting the 1929 German Probat roaster).[22]
- The next step (*relationships*) was much trickier; dread of the Starbucks juggernaut had crushed staff morale. Even worse, many staffers had wink-wink relationships with customers in which coffee and a bagel were ordered and provided, but only the coffee was paid for, while five dollars went into the tip jar. Sheldrake and Phibbs began Polly's reinvention by calling an all-hands meeting that started with (1) a graphic of the *Titanic* sinking, and (2) an announcement that all "special" customer relationships (otherwise known as theft) would stop immediately. Two employees walked out of the meeting and all but one of the remaining staff quit in short order. This presented a short-term crisis (somebody had to staff the store) but a long-term opportunity to build a new culture. Sheldrake took advantage by launching a training program for new employees that culminated in a one-hundred-question test confirming their knowledge of coffee and retail sales.[23]
- Sheldrake could offer no *security* in that moment of

reinvention; sales were plummeting, and everyone knew how difficult a competitor Starbucks would be. All he could offer were enthusiasm, hope, and commitment, along with a clear message that the apathy and woe-is-me-ism of the past had nearly killed Polly's. The only security possible for employees in the future lay in doing things differently now.

The results were dramatic: Polly's increased sales by 52 percent in its first year of reinvention, and 40 percent the next year. The store thrives to this day, now with an online coffee and accessory business too.[24]

Time Is Not Your Friend, Except When It Is

It's a rare change that is *less* urgent once its necessity is recognized. Yet human nature still tends toward hesitation and delay: "Faced with the choice between changing one's mind and proving that there is no need to do so," wrote economist John Kenneth Galbraith, "almost everyone gets busy on the proof."[25]

Get started today—as in, *now.* "Everybody has accepted by now that 'change is unavoidable,'" wrote management demigod Peter Drucker. "But this still implies that change is like 'death and taxes:' it should be postponed as long as possible, and no change would be vastly preferable. But in a period of upheavals, such as the one we are living in, change is the norm. To be sure, it is painful and risky, and above all, it requires a great deal of very hard work. But unless it is seen as the task of the organization to *lead change*, that organization—whether business, university, hospital and so on—will not survive."[26]

Please note, however, that the urgency is in getting change *started*, not in hurrying people through. "Time is necessary," wrote Lawrence, "even though there may be no resistance to the change itself . . . When staff people begin to lose patience with the amount of time that these steps take, the workers will begin to feel that they are being pushed; *this* amounts to a change in their customary work relationships, and resistance will start building up where there was none before."[27]

Carry the Wounded, but Shoot the Stragglers

All that said, after you have exhibited all the patience you can muster, at some point time is up, and change must happen— regardless of individual feelings or social statuses. You may not say it out loud, but in your head you need to make this commitment: carry the wounded, but shoot the stragglers. There are always those who cannot, or will not, change. As noted in chapter 3, under Mistakes and Unfixable Nincompoops: they have to go.

Aetna had to say goodbye to five thousand employees to survive. Polly's coffee needed all-but-one employee to leave to survive and thrive.

You can do this too.

You shouldn't feel great about it—these may (or may not) be fine people, they're losing jobs and colleagues—but you shouldn't feel guilty, either. Everyone makes a choice to change or not; your fiduciary and moral responsibility is to the organization and to those who (like you) are trying to move it forward. Here's how Jack Welch, GE's legendary CEO, explained it: "It sounds awful, but a crisis rarely ends without blood on the floor. That's not easy or pleasant. But sadly, it is often necessary so the company can move forward again."[28]

Fret, grieve, feel guilty, secretly high-five a colleague who's as fed up as you are, and then: *move.* Make the change swiftly and kindly, and then put it behind you. This will be easier than you think, because, just like the electric shock experiment, your anxiety about letting someone go is usually worse than the actual experience (especially with an underperformer or unrepentant pinhead). Now you can put your focus back where it belongs—on the final and biggest obstacle to change.

The Last and Biggest Obstacle to Change Is . . .

YOU.

Time and again I find that the biggest obstacle to leading change is the leader (in this case, you). Not because he or she is UNqualified, or UNmotivated, or UNpopular, or any of the other UNs you might think of; instead, they fall victim to the biggest UN of all: UNconfident.

This is the worst reason not to start or lead change.

Much of the time, when we fail to speak up, when we fail to take a chance that we know is reasonable, when we fail to make a change that we know will benefit our customers, our colleagues and employees, or our communities, it's because we doubt whether we are the right people to lead such a change. We all have a ready stock of terrible, self-limiting questions that we ask ourselves each time we face the challenge of starting something new:

- Haven't all the various flavors of nincompoops (including ourselves) pointed out why no sane person would lead such a change? (Of course they have, but that doesn't mean that they're right. After all, they're still acting like nincompoops.)
- Haven't we been trapped inside our own heads for so long that we're intimately acquainted with all of our many flaws, mistakes, and doubts, as well as the many ways that we have inadvertently or stupidly sabotaged ourselves or our companies over the years? (Of course we are, but experience—making mistakes and learning from them—doesn't disqualify you from leadership; it qualifies you.)
- Worst of all, haven't we managed to convince ourselves that all those flaws, insecurities, and known defects in competence and character are just as readily apparent to everyone else around us? (They are not, both because they're not as ugly and warty as you think, and also because everyone else is just as trapped in their own heads and their own insecurities as you are.)

In short, what possible reason do we have to believe that the naysayers—again, including ourselves—are wrong?

This is the fundamental question every leader faces before embarking upon change: apart from all the strategic planning, all the research, all the consensus-building and encouragement we give to others, do we believe enough in ourselves to try to make this happen?

A personal story is in order here. When I was thirty-four, after less than three years as a business journalist, I became an associate editor of *IndustryWeek* magazine (at that time, the "Bible" of manufacturing in the United States, with nearly 300,000 subscribers). Within six months, I had been promoted to executive editor and was tasked with developing a television show for the magazine, in partnership with CNBC. I had never been an executive editor before, or a manager of people at any profit-making organization; my complete experience in television had been limited to watching it. Yet I launched the show, and six months later, at age thirty-five, became editor-in-chief. Within three years—with the help of a supportive boss, talented colleagues, and some luck—we nearly tripled revenue, and went from losing some $1 million a year to making more than $2 million.

It's a happy story, with a happy ending. But it begs the question: Was I a secretly brilliant editor and manager, plucked from obscurity to reinvent business journalism, or at least *IndustryWeek*?

I wish.

During my job search before arriving at *IndustryWeek*, I was told by the business editor of a Pulitzer Prize-winning newspaper that I wasn't "ready to be an editor or manager, and needed more time as a reporter." (I didn't like hearing this, but he was probably right.) *IndustryWeek*, though, was failing (the magazine lost that same $1 million almost every year), with a disaffected staff in a declining market. The chairman of our parent company told us that we had less than a year to turn things around; my predecessor as editor-in-chief resigned to go elsewhere.

In other words, it's relatively easy to get a job with a title that sounds good, if very few people want it.

Fast forward to the day I was named editor-in-chief. I was both excited and nervous—how would we turn this around? Why on God's green earth did they (or anyone) believe that I could do this? What happens if (when) I fail, with a two-year-old at home and a mortgage I can barely afford?

In the midst of fretting and fantasizing, I received an unexpected visitor in my new office. He was an executive vice president with the company, and, through several layers of management, my new boss. I thought he had come to congratulate me, or to outline his vision of what I needed to do, or whatever it is that silver-haired EVPs in expensive suits do when you're a nincompoop who's just been promoted beyond your level of competence. But after the usual pleasantries, here's what he said: "Just so you know, everybody in this building thinks they can run this magazine better than you can."

I was taken aback. I already knew I was unqualified. What good did it do to rub it in?

I mean: What the hell?

But later, after I'd had a chance to turn those words over in my mind, I realized that he hadn't been taunting me, or emphasizing my youth and inexperience. Instead, in his own silver-haired-EVP way, he had given me a gift: I didn't need to listen to all the naysayers, the people who thought they knew more than me (many of them rightfully so), the people who *knew* that I would fail, because everyone else in the previous decade or so had failed too. Instead, he was giving me permission and approval to do something different—something, anything other than what all those smarter, better-qualified people *knew* would work.

So I did.

We outlined the urgency of becoming a new kind of media company to survive, and how that would require us to change everything: circulation, editorial focus, design, style, management, and technologies (*meaning*). We implemented a new culture of transparency, collaboration, decentralized management, and accountability (*relationships*). We couldn't offer current *security*—our chairman had been very clear about our tenuous position—so we focused instead on ensuring future security, by launching every new initiative we could think of: a CompuServe forum (cutting-edge in 1995), a website (also groovy in 1997), awards programs, an additional magazine, conferences, research studies, data products . . .

It was exhausting.

And exhilarating.

Most importantly, it was successful. We served readers and advertisers, we won seventy-plus editorial awards, we made money, and we had fun.

What more could you ask?

This transformation wasn't all or even mostly me, of course. Not by a longshot. But it did teach me that that I could be a leader, *if* I accepted that I didn't need to know everything, and that there would always be somebody smarter about every specific topic, or better at some specific task. I also learned that I didn't need to be the best at any one thing; instead, I needed to be somebody who understood how all those specific topics, tasks, and things worked in concert, and how to find the best people to think about or do or manage each one, and then how to get the best effort and outcome from everyone I worked with, regardless of personality or background . . .

Including me.

You Already Know Everything You Need to Know to Be a Leader

We started this book with a conviction: you already know everything you need to know to be a leader. We've covered what you need to do to lead change, and how to implement an Anti-Nincompoopery plan within your organization or team. We just discussed how worry about the nincompoopish opinions of others can hold us back, and why it shouldn't. So why do you (and me, much of the time) *still* feel like we're not ready, even when we are?

Some of it may be anxiety, or even humility, but more often than not it's also (or mostly) a lagging perception of who we are, and who we've become. If we haven't yet been a leader, if we haven't yet tried to do these things, if we can't yet see ourselves as leaders when we look in the mirror . . . how will anybody else?

This is the worst kind of Nincompoopery: the self-inflicted sort.

It doesn't have to be this way.

"Most people don't see themselves as leaders," said Herminia Ibarra, author of *Act Like a Leader, Think Like a Leader* and professor of organizational behavior at London Business School. "They don't have that as an identity or a label. Early in people's careers, most people's labels for themselves have to do with their technical skills or their professional training. They see themselves as an engineer, an accountant, a marketing specialist . . . They have in their minds unrealistic hero images of fantastic leaders or very negative images of the political manipulator or the bad boss. They are not so sure what it would really look like for them to lead." [29]

Ibarra also said that it's common to be unsure of what you're doing as you become a leader, and to worry that if you "fake it until you make it," you are somehow being dishonest or inauthentic (much like a young editor-in-chief I once knew): "In terms of career development, there's a tendency to hold onto a sense of authenticity that is constraining as opposed to expanding. People end up pigeonholing themselves . . . They think the *real* them is the past version, and that that basket of skills and preferences is what they're going to have the rest of their lives. That's not true. We evolve and change and develop new preferences . . . you can discover capacities you just didn't know you had because you were not in a role that allowed you to develop them."[30]

In other words, we somehow convince ourselves that we are still our previous inexperienced, nincompoopish selves—no matter how good our ideas are now, or how broad our experience is now, or how desperately our organizations need the change that we could provide now. We forget, too, the core truth underlying every successful plan to change, grow, and improve:

It's *never* the nincompoops, it's *always* the Nincompoopery.

Even if the nincompoops, until now, have included you or me.

So, one last time: You're more than ready to do this *now*. And only a nincompoop could *now* continue to ignore the Nincompoopery surrounding him-or herself.

What are you waiting for?

Anti-Nincompoopery Planning: You

Remember *This*.	Then Ask Yourself *This*!
You can always find somebody to tell you you're wrong.	Who on my team are members of: **The Woe is all of us club:** Nothing will ever change, and you are just wasting your time. **The Woe is you club:** You don't know enough, you've only been here for X years, etc. **The Woe is change club:** Okay, maybe that could work, and maybe I could even like that change, but . . . that would be hard. How could you/we ever do that?

Resistance to change is normal, and often healthy.	How can I create the conditions for change to be *possible*? How can I design incentives that make people more likely to *choose* change? How will I identify and remove those who actively *sabotage* change?
Big Requirement for Change #1 *Security.*	How will I communicate that the uncertain nature of change means that I will not be able to give everyone the answer they want *now*, which is how this will change their job in the *future*. How will I remain empathetic while being clear, concise, and transparent? How quickly can we make change happen?
Big Requirement for Change #2 *Relationships.*	How will I help my team manage the uncertainty that change brings into their lives? How will I help them manage this uncertainty *operationally*, *emotionally*, and *socially*? How can I create an environment in which employees can speak up, and feel heard and respected?
Big Requirement for Change #3 *Meaning.*	How will I outline a compelling need for change, and an equally compelling vision of what the future will look like? What will the change *be*, what it will *require*, and what will the *future state look like*? What are the values and principles by which we will live as change happens (such as transparency, inclusiveness, commitment to principles, etc.)?
The last and biggest obstacle to change is *You*.	Do I believe enough in *myself* to lead this change? If not, why?
You already know everything you need to know to be a leader.	What am I waiting for? Why?

Nincompoopery Macro Trends:

Why Is It So Ridiculously Hard to Be a Leader These Days?

What Is Success?

Let's start with this: character, goodwill, persistence, pluck, optimism, and cheerfulness—along with a healthy dose of luck—will go a long way toward making you a personal success. Many a silver-haired executive has risen to the top based on a dazzling smile and a pleasant disposition, even if he wasn't the best or brightest (in other words, he was a nincompoop). As Justice Oliver Wendell Holmes, Jr. said of President Theodore Roosevelt: "A second-class intellect, but a first-class temperament."[1]

Yet *personal* success is not the same as leading and inspiring *organizational* success. We all know nincompoops, ninnies, and nitwits who have done well for themselves, but whose organizations have failed.

Leading an Organization (Without Being a Nincompoop) Has Never Been More Challenging

Alas, it is fundamentally more difficult to lead an organization today than ever before. Which means, of course, it also far harder to avoid Nincompoopery, due to six Big Leadership Trends.

Big Leadership Trend #1: We are in the middle of a very long, very strange economic recovery that has fundamentally altered the psychological outlook of business leaders.

Manufacturing led this recovery, but not because manufacturing executives are smarter, bolder, or more prescient than leaders in other industries; they overachieved simply because their revenues had fallen so precipitously in 2008 and 2009 that they had nowhere to go but up. In fact, firms in many sectors have only recently seen revenues return to pre-Great Recession levels, and still lack pricing power. Executives may well look at their numbers and think: *It's nice that times are better, but when can we improve margins and profitability?*

The result of this uncertainty has been that even as the economy improved, many leaders remained reluctant to invest heavily in new equipment or systems, or in additional hiring (leading to the long period of "jobless recovery" cited by many commentators). Although these concerns are receding, executives who lived through the Great Recession may be psychologically scarred for the rest of their careers, much like so-called Depression Babies, who grew up in the 1930s and were permanently averse to risk, based on the memory of how badly things can go wrong.

It's a Tough, Strange Time to Be a Leader

And that's just the effect of the last few years. Longer-term changes in the economy have made leadership even more difficult. The economy has evolved dramatically within our lifetimes; just after World War II, for example, roughly 34 percent of all US workers toiled in manufacturing plants or on farms; today, barely 12 percent do. The service sector absorbed (and then multiplied) nearly all those jobs—rising from 13 percent of total employment to 30 percent. But, and this is an enormous *but*, manufacturing as a sector didn't shrink; as measured by output, it's actually six times bigger. How? By becoming more efficient—via automation, information technology, better logistics, and improvement methodologies such as Lean or Six Sigma—and requiring fewer workers for vastly higher levels of production. These same forces improved productivity (and drove growth in output) even faster in service sectors such as management consulting, health care, education, marketing, and others.[2] Managing in an era of accelerating change—when new ideas and business models can emerge quickly from anywhere around the globe, undermining established market positions—is a challenge unprecedented in business history.

Information Technology Has Rewired the Competitive Landscape

Big Leadership Trend #2: A data-fueled productivity explosion has profoundly impacted labor markets and employees.

The number of internet users reached 3.9 billion in 2018, roughly half the world's population.[3] Facebook now has more than 2 billion users,[4] and the number of tweets sent per day is 500 million.[5] Connectivity and the ability to mine insights from a data-rich environment—whether those insights are collected via web browsing, email, or social media—are vital components of productivity and innovation in the twenty-first century. A requirement for employees who can assimilate, interpret, and act upon a continuous flow of information is reflected in statistics about who's gained ground, and who's lost it, in labor markets. Over the last fifty years, earning a college degree has become more important than ever; over that period, college-educated men saw real increases in their median incomes of 22 percent. Conversely, every group of men with less education saw real incomes decline. And while all groups of women saw real incomes increase, thanks to reduced discrimination, college-educated women enjoyed increases of more than 50 percent. If you want to get ahead personally, or if you want your company to do well, you and your employees need to get smarter. And fast.[6]

At the same time, the easy ubiquity afforded to knowledge work via information technology—combined with lower trade restrictions and advances in logistics—have revolutionized where business happens as well. In 2012 the BRIC economies (Brazil,

156

Russia, India, and China) comprised almost 25 percent of global output; that number could rise to 33 percent by 2020.[7] Indeed, many believe that global economic growth will be concentrated in emerging economies by 2025, with six nations (Brazil, China, India, Indonesia, Korea, and Russia) contributing more than half of all growth worldwide.[8] Leaders have to wonder where they should do business next year, and a decade from now, to maximize profitability (or just survive).

Global Demographics Are Changing the Nature of the Workforce

Big Leadership Trend #3: Workforce demographics are rapidly changing thanks to improved health care and longevity.

Even as the world's population rises 7 percent between 2010 and 2020, reaching 7.6 billion people, the number of *available* employees (that is, of working age) will actually decline in many industrialized nations. Japan has already hit this retirement tipping point; Europe began seeing retirements outstrip the number of new workforce entrants in 2010. This is a major concern for leaders, because nearly a third of companies already find it hard to fill positions due to talent shortages.[9]

This demographic tsunami may loom even larger and be even more sweeping in its effects in the United States. During this decade alone (2010–2020), more than twenty-five million American workers will leave the workforce permanently, while thirty-six million join. Yet remaining baby boomers will make the entire workface older, dragging its median age up to 42.8 years in 2020 versus just 36.4 in 1990.[10] In fact, every baby boomer will be fifty-six or older by 2020, and some will be seventy-four. Why are they sticking around? Mostly because they're healthier than previous generations, but also because they're scared. Longevity is a double-edged sword; it's nice to enjoy more years, but you have to be able to pay for them. Almost half of boomers plan to wait until sixty-six or later to retire, and 10 percent say they never will.[11] Overall, some 43 percent of people over fifty-five will still be working in 2020—a massive increase over the 32.4 percent who did so in 1990.

And the workforce of the future will look increasingly different than today. People of color already accounted for 36 percent of the US labor force in 2012; by 2050, the United States will be a nation of ethnic pluralities, because no group will be a majority. Women already comprise nearly half of US workers, and that percentage will continue to rise.[12] Leaders who want the best results will have to rethink how they find, train, compensate, and retain the best talent—regardless of age, color, or gender.

Employee Expectations Are Changing

Big Leadership Trend #4: Employees also have different expectations for how their work life is structured and managed in a digital era.

With more than six billion smartphones projected worldwide by 2020,[13] we've reached a moment of digital saturation among the workforce, at least in developed countries. We have succeeded in creating an environment in which our employees can, if they wish or we demand, work 24/7—and they are, with some checking their phones as many as 150 times per day.[14]

We and they should be more productive, thanks to all this connectivity, but new research says we're not, and that the biggest lie we've sold ourselves is the myth of increased productivity via multitasking. In fact, we lose up to 40 percent of our productivity by switching between tasks;[15] the more we switch, the worse our performance. Why? Mainly because our brains are overwhelmed by data and information. In just one example, participation in a 401(k) program falls dramatically as the number of available options increases—from 75 percent when there are two investment options, to just 61 percent when there are fifty-nine options. Even sadder, whenever participants in a plan have more options, they tend to make worse choices, picking investments with lower returns.[16]

It turns out that the human brain can only hold about seven items at one time.[17] When digital temptations abound—57 percent of interruptions at work come from switching between different types of software or social media[18]—we not only lose track of what we're doing, we feel guilty about it. A recent study of knowledge workers found that they wasted 41 percent of their time on tasks that didn't move work or projects forward—and that they despised.[19]

That's why some senior executives and professionals are trying schedule quiet (that is, nonelectronic) time for themselves each day, to promote a quaint concept we used to call *thinking*. Some companies have tried to go further, issuing draconian mandates regarding email-free work periods; these rarely worked, in part because they didn't respect individual work schedules and preferences (some people feel more productive in the morning, others in the afternoon or evening). A more promising trend is illustrated by Daimler, the German automaker; employees leaving the office can set their company email to "holiday mode." When they do, incoming emails receive an automated response directing the sender to an alternate contact and then the incoming email is deleted. Workers return from "holiday mode" to email inboxes that look the same as when they left, with no mountain of responses or guilt to manage.[20]

And yet, as Shakespeare wrote, the fault lies not in our stars (or corporate email systems), but in ourselves. As much as we curse our digital distractions, we expect—demand—to be connected continuously, across the entire range of electronic media. This has created heartburn for leaders: How do we simultaneously respect our employees' desire to be connected while also recognizing the productivity issues that ensue, as well as the reputational and confidentiality risks posed by employee use of social media?

The first, knee-jerk reaction of many executives to this question was to ban corporate use of social media by anyone other than the marketing team. Other leaders, however, saw more opportunity than risk. Mastercard, for example, found that employees wanted to connect to the rest of their lives outside the office—whether by ordering dinner online or staying in touch with friends via social media. Instead of running from the challenge (Mastercard has much to fear from accidental disclosures of financial or customer information), the company launched a social media training program for employees. In essence, the company accepted that employees are on social media, so it's better to teach them how to safeguard sensitive information while leveraging opportunities for employees to collaborate internally and become brand representatives externally. The detailed training plan included a "reverse mentorship" program, in which younger employees tutored senior executives on how to use social media.[21]

Evolving employee expectations go well beyond the digital realm, however. It's not uncommon, for instance, to hear a senior executive say (if he or she thinks nobody under forty is listening) something along the lines of: "This younger generation, they just don't want to work. They don't have a work ethic." In one sense, this is the same thing that every generation says about the ones that follow: they're lazy, they don't know how good they've got it, their music is terrible, etc. And yet this reflexive dismissal of millennials (those born after 1980) is more unfair than usual, given that they were the first generation in history to have detailed schedules *as kids*—preschool, play dates, sports, travel teams, dance, enrichment classes, and so forth. In fact, millennials can make a strong case that they've been working since age three, and that they're better prepared for the workplace than any previous generation.

This is a tremendous opportunity for leaders and companies, since by 2025 millennials will make up three quarters of the global workforce.[22] Yet it's also a challenge, because millennials are not only digitally savvier than previous generations, but also want different things from work. And while generational differences in the workforce aren't as simple as some consultants would have you believe—

- Baby boomers supposedly love to work hard, but miss out on life.
- Gen Xers (born 1965–1980) supposedly think baby boomers are losers, and focus their attention on their own quality of life.

- Millennials supposedly think Xers are slackers for not caring *enough* about work, and look for flexibility and work-life balance.

—savvy companies such as General Electric have formed task forces to better engage millennials socially and digitally, with options such as cafeteria benefit plans, improved career coaching, and the use of gaming technology in training.[23]

The Social Contract of Employment Is Changing

Big Leadership Trend #5: These economic and social trends have also led to fundamental changes in the social contract between employers and employees.

In the United States, there was a brief (in historical terms) period after World War II during which some (white male) workers could reasonably expect that if they worked hard, avoided trouble, and agreed to modest raises, their employers would take care of them for life, including retirement plans and medical benefits. The reality was never actually that simple or secure—and vast swaths of the population were never included in any way, most notably women and people of color—but the idea of an implied cradle-to-grave employment contract became embedded in the American psyche.

And then the world changed.

Economic activity accelerated dramatically; the average life expectancy of an S&P 500 company used to be seventy-five years, but today it's fifteen years.[24] Why? As the 1973 oil crisis, recessions, and stagflation torpedoed corporate bottom lines, companies began mass permanent layoffs in the late 1970s and early 1980s—shattering communities and the social contract between employees and employers. Parents began telling their children: "You cannot count on a company to take care of you for the rest of your life. You must take care of yourself, and the only security you will ever have are the skills you carry in your head."

Against all odds, and despite how it looked every time they rolled their eyes, the kids listened and understood. The numbers prove it: Gen Xers and millennials are likely to have anywhere from seven to ten jobs during their careers, often in vastly different industries.[25] This means that when a smart member of these generations analyzes an employment opportunity, he or she isn't looking for a lifetime commitment from either side. Instead, he or she is asking: "What can I learn at this organization? Is this a good environment in which to work? Will opportunities here add to my portfolio of skills and make me more secure in the long term?"

This means that leaders must ask themselves: "Why should an employee be loyal to us, if we can't guarantee loyalty to them in the long term?"

Many leaders are finding that the answer is to become an employer of choice, by offering not just opportunity and competitive wages but intangible incentives as well. Can we offer a great work environment, in which purpose and respect are the foundations of corporate culture? Given the prevalence of dual-income and single-parent households, can we offer flexible work schedules or part-time work? These intangibles require fundamental changes in how organizations are managed, but are vital in attracting, leveraging, and retaining talent. Research from

Gallup says just 20 percent of employees in the United States are "happy."[26] This is a silent crisis within many companies, because unhappy workers are far more likely to leave; 58 percent of "generally dissatisfied" workers plan to leave their jobs within a year.[27] On the flip side, quality-of-work-life programs help significantly; employees in a formal mentorship program have a 23 percent higher retention rate.[28] Tuition reimbursement programs are even more effective, doubling the likelihood that employees stay.[29]

Customers Are Demanding More than Ever

Big Leadership Trend #6: A rapid increase in official and de facto regulations across international, national, and regional jurisdictions in recent years has significantly complicated leadership.

In the automotive sector, for example, US corporate average fuel economy (CAFE) standards will require an average fuel economy of 54.5 miles per gallon in 2025.[30] (Note: The US Environmental Protection Agency and Department of Transportation have proposed a rollback of CAFE standards, which would freeze fuel efficiencies at 2020 levels, roughly thirty-seven miles per gallon.)[31] More and more companies also find themselves subject to international regulations, such as European Union traceability-by-lot food regulations or the General Data Protection Regulation (GDPR). State and local ordinances such as the California Citrus Program,[32] which sets standards for orange maturity and citrus freeze damage, also complicate record-keeping and compliance.

Yet official regulations are just the tip of the iceberg. Customers have always wanted more each year (improved features, better service, lower prices, etc.) But now corporations find themselves subjected to even greater demands, in the form of *de facto* regulations by which customers say: "Thanks for the great product. But you also have to comply with our policies, in this way, with this documentation, because we have to guarantee the reputations of our company and our suppliers (i.e., *you*)." What's more, major customers such as Walmart, General Electric, or Nike often require compliance with ethical or sustainability standards that exceed those of government regulations. This has been driven both by evolving executive consciences and by the new visibility of bad business behavior via targeted media campaigns. The National Labor Committee, for example—with only a few staff members—changed the way the apparel industry sourced clothing, by focusing attention on brands that bought from factories using unsafe or child labor in Third World countries; other campaigns targeted toy and automotive manufacturers.[33] Digital and social media have also made ordinary consumers more powerful than ever, via reviews on sites such as Yelp, TripAdvisor, or Amazon; 80 percent of irritated customers stop buying after a single bad experience, and 82 percent tell everybody they know.[34]

Social media initiatives are even more effective at influencing corporate behavior. Greenpeace used a Facebook campaign to target Nestlé for its use of Indonesian palm oil from growers suspected of illegally cutting down endangered rainforests. (Greenpeace drove the cause with a viral video of a cubicle dweller who thought he was eating a Kit Kat, only to discover that it was an orangutan finger.) Nestlé quickly pledged to stop using the oil in Kit Kats.[35] And it's not just multinationals that are at risk: Demoulas Super Markets Inc., a New England chain, saw a board dispute among family members turn into a full-blown crisis after more than thirteen thousand people signed an online petition urging a boycott, leading to falling sales and empty shelves before the situation was resolved.[36]

It's No Wonder Leaders Feel Overwhelmed

Leaders understand that their role is to create sustainable value and profits. Yet many think about the challenges above and other industry-specific issues, and ask: "Sustainable? What about survival? How can we possibly be competitive tomorrow, much less in ten years?"

These are reasonable questions. In sector after sector, old-school economics no longer work. Take advertising and media, for example: by 2014, 48 percent of all video watched in the United States was already time-or device-shifted (that is, viewed on DVR or via on-demand services, or on some type of mobile device). If your main product is advertising, how do you adjust? And it's not just video: by 2014, tablets and phones were already used for 44 percent of all personal computing time (phones, in fact, were used only 20 percent of the time for voice-to-voice communication), with 25 percent of that time spent on social networking. Where does advertising fit in this brave new world? And this tectonic shift occurred over less than a decade, leaving traditional media companies, and the sponsors that rely upon them, gasping for breath.[37]

Fortunately, There's Hope and a Formula for Success

We started this afterword by noting that *personal* success is vastly easier and more common than effective leadership of *organizational* success.

But there is hope.

In chapter 1 (page **XX**), we sketch out an Anti-Nincompoopery plan that relies on three broad cultural and operational strategies:

- **Innovation:** Are you developing, making, and delivering new value that meets stakeholder needs at a pace faster than the competition? (See chapter 2.)
- **Talent:** Are you achieving competitive advantage by having superior systems in place to recruit, hire, develop, and retain the best talent? (See chapter 3.)
- **Process:** Are you recording annual productivity and quality gains that exceed those of competitors through an organization-wide commitment to continuous improvement? (See chapter 4.)

These strategies have worked for companies of every size, in every industry, with leaders at every level of experience (see chapter 5). They'll work for you, too, if you're open to change and are willing to lead your team, location, unit, or company away from the self-inflicted foolishness of Nincompoopery and toward a better future. Why?

1. First, as an effective, non-nincompoop leader, you'll shrink the 41 percent of time spent by yourself and your

colleagues on meaningless, irritating tasks by focusing instead on *inspiring employees to invest more time, effort, and money into fostering greatness within each strategy.*

2. More importantly, you'll *manage all the strategies in ways that differ significantly from competitors.* You'll make sure that your company implements best practices at far higher rates than rival firms.

3. Finally, you'll *deploy measurements and metrics across the strategies far more creatively than your competitors,* to make sure that customers, employees, and suppliers are more productive, engaged, and happy.

Oh, and this: you will have far more fun, and make far more money for your company.

Let's GO!

Anti-Nincompoopery Planning: Why Is It So Ridiculously Hard to Be a Leader These Days?

Remember *This*.	Then Ask Yourself *This*!
Big Leadership Trend #1 We are in the middle of a very long, very strange economic recovery that has fundamentally altered the psychological outlook of business leaders.	Is our team or company averse to risk or change? Is our team or company ready to manage in an era of accelerating change—when new ideas and business models can emerge quickly from anywhere around the globe, undermining established market positions?
Big Leadership Trend #2 A data-fueled productivity explosion has profoundly impacted labor markets and employees.	Have we found and trained employees who can assimilate, interpret, and act upon a continuous flow of information? Which regions and markets will innovations in data-fueled productivity allow us to enter? Are we leveraging technology to optimize profitability?
Big Leadership Trend #3 Workforce demographics are rapidly changing, thanks to improved health care and longevity.	How will we find the talent we need as baby boomers retire and skills shortages increase? How will we find, train, compensate, and retain the best talent—regardless of age, color, or gender?
Big Leadership Trend #4 Employees have different expectations for how their work lives are structured and managed in a digital era.	How will we create a productive environment with healthy boundaries and balance between employees' work and personal lives? How will we make sure technology improves focus, creativity, and productivity? How can we leverage social media to connect meaningfully with employees, customers, and other stakeholders?

Big Leadership Trend #5 These economic and social trends have also led to fundamental changes in the social contract between employers and employees.	If we can no longer offer lifetime employment and pensions, what can we offer as a new social contract to employees? How can we become an employer of choice? Which specific benefits could benefit both employees *and* our company (e.g., training, tuition reimbursement, formal mentorship programs)?
Big Leadership Trend #6 A rapid increase in official and *de facto* regulations across international, national, and regional jurisdictions in recent years has significantly complicated leadership.	How will we manage the increasing complexity and cost of compliance with official and *de facto* rules, regulations, and requirements? How will we ensure that our company meets not only explicit regulatory requirements but implicit moral and reputational requirements too?

Acknowledgments

There's a lot of Nincompoopery involved in writing a book, most (or all) of it self-inflicted. Starts and stops, grandiose visions (this could change *everything*) and moments of despair (I will *never* finish this), administrivial errors (where *is* that source?) . . . it's never as straightforward as it should be, or at least as it *seems* it should be.

Still, if a would-be author (and confirmed nincompoop) is lucky enough to find himself encouraged and abetted by angels of better natures than his own, he may persevere and finish the damn thing, and perhaps even publish it. That certainly happened with this book, and I am unreservedly grateful to the following angels, without whom this particular form of *Nincompoopery* would never have seen the light of day:

- My parents, Patricia and Reynold Brandt, and sister Karen, who encouraged me to pursue my own path. (Reynold: "There's always room at the top.")
- My children, Emma and Aidan Brandt. Emma completed much of the research, edited the first draft, provided vital (if occasionally unwelcome) feedback, and encouraged me

to choose, as a theme and title, "Nincompoopery"; Aidan also provided valuable research and feedback. More importantly, these two wickedly smart, delightfully kind human beings also keep me honest in writing and life, calling me out for various forms of idiocy while still gracing me with unconditional love.

- My ex-wife, Lana Brandt, who made it possible early in our marriage for me to leave a comfortable job and pursue a career in business journalism (at half my then-current salary). Her exact words, I believe, when I told her I would likely turn down an offer to go back into journalism were: "Are you out of your——-mind? You've been happier in the last year than you have been for the last ten."

- Richard Osborne, who made the job offer above, and who taught me how to be a real reporter and a more graceful writer.

- George Taninecz, MPI's vice president of research, who crafted *Nincompoopery*'s outline from a long speech I gave at a conference. His critical thinking and quiet support make every project, and every day, better.

- The Arcardians (my writing group), consisting of Mark McConville, Ed Walsh, and Jim Wood. This lot patiently waited twenty-one years for me to finish something of significance. I did buy them a lot of coffee though.

- Alec Pendleton, whose review of the first draft gave *Nincompoopery* the benefit of both his experience in fixing businesses and his touch with language. Also, the Manhattans were tasty.

- My agent, Linda Konner, who responded within ten minutes to my query letter, and made sure this book got published.

- The team at HarperCollins Leadership, including vice president and publisher Jeff James, senior acquisitions editor Tim Burgard, and editor Amanda Bauch, all of whom made this a more intelligent book via thoughtful critiques and gentle edits; marketing and publicity experts Hiram Centeno and Sicily Axton, who made sure readers could find the book; and a host of others who made it possible for *Nincompoopery* to appear in your hands.
- The Martini Golf League, whose members provide both adolescent humor and unwavering support for the only English major they know.
- Shelley Freed, who believed in the book but, more importantly, in me.

Thank you all.

Notes

Chapter 2

1. Carmen Nobel, "Clay Christensen's Milkshake Marketing," Harvard Business School Working Knowledge, February 14, 2011, https://hbswk.hbs.edu/item/clay-christensens-milkshake-marketing.

2. Mark Boroush, "NSF Releases New Statistics on Business Innovation," National Science Foundation, Division of Science Resources Statistics, October 2010, https://wayback.archive-it.org/5902/20150628150948/http://www.nsf.gov/statistics/infbrief/nsf11300/nsf11300.pdf.

3. Henry G. Grabowski and Ronald W. Hansen, "Innovation in the Pharmaceutical Industry: New Estimates of R&D Costs," Tufts Center for the Study of Drug Development, November 18, 2014, accessed February 1, 2019, https://static1.squarespace.com/static/5a9eb0c8e2ccd1158288d8dc/t/5ac66afc6d2a732e83aae6bf/1522952963800/Tufts_CSDD_briefing_on_RD_cost_study_-_Nov_18%2C_2014.pdf.

4. "Why P&G's Smile Is So Bright," *Bloomberg Businessweek*, August 11, 2002, https://www.bloomberg.com/news/articles/2002-08-11/why-p-and-gs-smile-is-so-bright.

5. "Statistics of U.S. Businesses (SUSB)," United States Census Bureau, 2012, https://www.census.gov/programs-surveys/susb.html.

6. James Robinson, "The Simple Truth of Nike's FuelBand Retreat Is That It Just Wasn't Very Good," Pando, April 21, 2014, https://pando.com/2014/04/21/the-simple-truth-of-nikes-fuelband-retreat-is-that-it-just-wasnt-very-good/.

7. Joan Schneider and Julie Hall, "Why Most Product Launches Fail," *Harvard Business Review*, April 2011, https://hbr.org/2011/04/why-most-product-launches-fail.

8. Leslie Kaufman, "Barnes & Noble Weighs Its E-Reader Investment," *The New York Times*, February 24, 2013, https://www.nytimes.com/2013/02/25/business/media/barnes-noble-weighs-its-nook-losses.html.

9. *Merriam-Webster*, s.v. "innovate (*v.*)," accessed December 15, 2018, https://www.merriam-webster.com/dictionary/innovate.

10. Michael DeGusta, "Are Smart Phones Spreading Faster than Any Technology in Human History?" *MIT Technology Review*, May 9, 2012, https://www.technologyreview.com/s/427787/are-smart-phones-spreading-faster-than-any-technology-in-human-history/.

11. Bill Powell, "360buy's Qiangdong Liu: China's New E-commerce Star," *Fortune*, October 14, 2011, http://fortune.com/2011/10/14/360buys-qiangdong-liu-chinas-new-e-commerce-star/.

12. Powell, "360buy's Qiangdong Liu."

13. Frank Tong, "Alibaba's Chief Competitor Gets a Big Edge in Selling to Young Chinese Shoppers," *Internet Retailer*, August 12, 2014, https://www.digitalcommerce360.com/2014/08/12/alibabas-chief-competitor-gets-big-edge/.

14. Now known as *Guinness World Records*.

15. Mallory Russell, "250 Years of Genius: A Look at the Evolution of Guinness Advertising," Business Insider, March 12, 2012, https://www.businessinsider.com/an-evolution-of-guinness-advertising-2012–3.

16. Scott Kirsner, "Brand Marketing: Guinness," *Fast Company*, April 30, 2002, https://www.fastcompany.com/44736/brand-marketing-guinness.

17. Kirsner, "Brand Marketing: Guinness."

18.

19. Kirsner, "Brand Marketing: Guinness."

20. Gemma Charles, "Q&A: Guinness Global Strategy and Communications Director Grainne Wafer," *Campaign*, October 29, 2012, https://www.campaignlive.co.uk/article/q-a-guinness-global-strategy-communications-director-grainne-wafer/1156974.

21. Jerry Lieber and Mike Stoller, "Is That All There Is?" Capitol Records, 1969 (Peggy Lee version).

22. Stuart Whitwell, "Ingredient Branding Case Study: Intel," Intangible Business, November 2005, available at https://www.scribd.com/document/43316770/360-Ingredient-Branding-Case-Study-Intel.

23. The MPI Group, "Manufacturing 2015: The Return of Profitability," 2015, https://mpi-group.com/wp-content/uploads/2015/05/Manufacturing-2015-Executive-Summary-LOCK.pdf.

24. David Drickhamer, "Lean Management Case Study Series: Lean In Distribution: Go to Where the Action Is!" Lean Enterprise Institute, November 29, 2012, https://www.lean.org/common/display/?o=2179.

25. "Beau-coup Makes the Search for Wedding Favors a Piece of Cake," UPS, 2012, https://www.ups.com/media/en/Beau_coup_case_study.pdf.

26. Henry Chesbrough, "Open Services Innovation," Innovation Excellence, November 4, 2012, https://www.innovationexcellence.com/blog/2012/11/04/open-services-innovation/.

27. Tina Nielsen, "How to Work with Big Companies to Grow a Small Business," *The Guardian*, August 20, 2013, https://www.theguardian.com/small-business-network/2013/aug/20/big-company-partnership-grow-small-business.

28. "Our Story," Green Tomato Cars, www.greentomatocars.com/en-uk/about.

29. Kipp Bodnar, "Generating Small Business Customers with Social Media Marketing," HubSpot, accessed January 31, 2019,

https://blog.hubspot.com/blog/tabid/6307/bid/5976/Free-eBook-Generating-Small-Business-Customers-With-Social-Media.aspx.

30. Stefan Thomke and Eric von Hippel, "Customers as Innovators: A New Way to Create Value," *Harvard Business Review*, April 2002, https://hbr.org/2002/04/customers-as-innovators-a-new-way-to-create-value.

31. Brittany W., "Crowdsourcing Your Next Chip Flavor: Lay's "Do Us A Flavor" Campaign," Digital Innovation and Transformation: A Course at Harvard Business School, March 24, 2018, https://digit.hbs.org/submission/crowdsourcing-your-next-chip-flavor-lays-do-us-a-flavor-campaign/#.

32. David Kirkpatrick, "B2B Crowdsourcing: Product Development Effort Boosts Sales 17 Percent and New Product Sales 37 Percent," MarketingSherpa, February 15, 2012, https://www.marketingsherpa.com/article/case-study/product-development-effort-boosts-sales.

33. Christopher Wasden and Brian Williams, "Owning the Disease: A New Transformational Business Model for Healthcare," PwC, 2011, https://www.pwc.com/il/en/pharmaceuticals/assets/owning-the-disease.pdf.

34. Danielle Beurteaux, "Same-Day Delivery Resurges, Adding Alcohol," *The New York Times*, February 18, 2015, https://www.nytimes.com/2015/02/19/business/smallbusiness/same-day-delivery-resurges-adding-alcohol.html.

35. Andy Reinhardt, "Steve Jobs: 'There's Sanity Returning,'" *BusinessWeek*, May 25, 1998, http://www.businessweek.com/1998/21/b3579165.htm.

36. Meaghan Haire, "A Brief History of the Walkman," *Time*, July 1, 2009, http://content.time.com/time/nation/article/0,8599,1907884,00.html.

37. Steve McCallion, "How Customers Saying 'No' Can Become a Consumer Experience 'Yes,'" *Fast Company*, August 19, 2009, https://www.fastcompany.com/1331829/how-customers-saying-no-can-become-consumer-experience-yes.

38. Lindsey Kratochwill, "Not Your Grandma's Knitting Circle," *Bloomberg BusinessWeek*, September 24, 2015,

https://www.bloomberg.com/news/articles/2015–09–24/
wool-the-gang-not-your-grandma-s-knitting-circle.

39. Crowdcube, "Over £5 Has Been Returned to Investors,"
August 30, 2016, https://www.crowdcube.com/explore/investor/
over-5-million-has-been-returned-to-investors.

40. Wool and the Gang, "WATG Are Crowdfunding," September
15, 2015, https://www.woolandthegang.com/blog/2015/09/
watg-are-crowdfunding.

41. Procter & Gamble, 2018 Annual Report, p. 11,
http://www.pginvestor.com/Cache/1001242072.
PDF?O=PDF&T=&Y=&D=&FID=1001242072&iid=4004124.

42. A.G. Lafley and Ram Charan, "The Consumer Is Boss," *Fortune*,
March 10, 2008, http://archive.fortune.com/2008/03/07/news/
companies/lafley_charan.fortune/index.htm.

43. Phil Drew, "Clash of the Titans: How Collaboration
Got Competitive," *The Guardian*, November 21, 2012,
https://www.theguardian.com/sustainable-business/blog/
titans-collaboration-competitive-business.

44. John Grossman, "A Seasonal Business Aims to Survive the Off-
Season," *The New York Times*, July 11, 2012, https://www.
nytimes.com/2012/07/12/business/smallbusiness/a-seasonal-
business-aims-to-survive-the-off-season.html.

45. Joseph Pisani, "A Customer Yelps; a Small Business Owner
Helps," Yahoo! Small Business, October 26, 2012, https://
smallbusiness.yahoo.com/advisor/customer-yelps-small-business-
owner-helps-150403947.html.

Chapter 3

1. *Merriam-Webster*, s.v. "talent (*n.*)," accessed December 15, 2018,
https://www.merriam-webster.com/dictionary/talent.

2. Rachel Gillett, "Infographic: How Much a Bad Hire
Will Actually Cost You," *Fast Company*, April 8,
2014, https://www.fastcompany.com/3028628/
infographic-how-much-a-bad-hire-will-actually-cost-you.

3. Allie Bidwell, "Report: Economy Will Face Shortage of 5
Million Workers in 2020," *U.S. News & World Report*, July 8,

2013, https://www.usnews.com/news/articles/2013/07/08/
report-economy-will-face-shortage-of-5-million-workers-in-2020.

4. Mamta Badkar, "Labor Shortages Will Cost the World
   $10 Trillion," *Business Insider*, July 1, 2014, https://www.
   businessinsider.com/labor-shortages-will-cost-10-trillion-2014–7.

5. Jenny Cermak and Monica McGurk, "Putting a Value on
   Training," *McKinsey Quarterly*, July 2010, https://www.
   mckinsey.com/business-functions/organization/our-insights/
   putting-a-value-on-training.

6. Cermak and McGurk, "Putting a Value on Training."

7. Rachel Emma Silverman, "So Much Training, So Little to Show
   for It," *The Wall Street Journal*, October 26, 2012, https://www.
   wsj.com/articles/SB1000142405297020442590457807295051855
   8328.

8. Marc Beaujean, Jonathan Davidson, and Stacy Madge,
   "The 'Moment of Truth' in Customer Service," *McKinsey
   Quarterly*, February 2006, https://www.mckinsey.
   com/business-functions/organization/our-insights/
   the-moment-of-truth-in-customer-service.

9. Beaujean, Davidson, and Madge, "'Moment of Truth.'"

10. Beaujean, Davidson, and Madge, "'Moment of Truth.'"

11. Southwest Airlines Co., "Southwest Airlines Reports Fourth
    Quarter and Record Annual Profit; 44th Consecutive Year of
    Profitability," PR Newswire, January 26, 2017, https://www.
    prnewswire.com/news-releases/southwest-airlines-reports-fourth-
    quarter-and-record-annual-profit-44th-consecutive-year-of-
    profitability-300397175.html.

12. Shawn Tully, "Southwest Bets Big on Business Travelers,"
    Fortune, September 23, 2015, http://fortune.com/2015/09/23/
    southwest-airlines-business-travel/.

13. Julie Weber, "How Southwest Airlines Hires Such
    Dedicated People," *Harvard Business Review*,
    December 2, 2015, https://hbr.org/2015/12/
    how-southwest-airlines-hires-such-dedicated-people.

14. Weber, "How Southwest Airlines Hires."

15. Atul Gawande, "The Hot Spotters: Can We Lower Medical

Costs by Giving the Neediest Patients Better Care?" *The New Yorker*, January 24, 2011, https://www.newyorker.com/magazine/2011/01/24/the-hot-spotters.

16. Gawande, "The Hot Spotters."
17. Gawande, "The Hot Spotters."
18. Gawande, "The Hot Spotters."
19. IR.Hertz.com, Corporate Governance, accessed January 31, 2019, http://ir.hertz.com/corporate-governance.
20. Vanessa Flynn, "Hertz Drives Standardized Talent Acquisition," *Talent Management*, January 30, 2011.
21. Flynn, "Hertz Drives Standardized Talent Acquisition."
22. Flynn, "Hertz Drives Standardized Talent Acquisition."
23. Flynn, "Hertz Drives Standardized Talent Acquisition."
24. Bill Taylor, "How One Fast-Food Chain Keeps Its Turnover Rates Absurdly Low," *Harvard Business Review*, January 26, 2016, https://hbr.org/2016/01/how-one-fast-food-chain-keeps-its-turnover-rates-absurdly-low.
25. Taylor, "How One Fast-Food Chain."
26. Taylor, "How One Fast-Food Chain."
27. Taylor, "How One Fast-Food Chain."
28. Taylor, "How One Fast-Food Chain."
29. Taylor, "How One Fast-Food Chain."
30. Taylor, "How One Fast-Food Chain."
31. David Drickhamer, "Open Book Management: By the Numbers," *Material Handling & Logistics*, January 1, 2006, https://www.mhlnews.com/facilities-management/open-book-management-numbers.
32. Robert Half Management Resources, "Most Private Companies Don't Update Staff on Financial Performance," August 28, 2012, http://rh-us.mediaroom.com/2012–08–28-Most-Private-Companies-Dont-Update-Staff-on-Financial-Performance.
33. Robert Half Management Resources, "Most Private Companies Don't Update Staff."
34. "The U.S. Illiteracy Rate Hasn't Changed in 10 Years," *The Huffington Post*, September 6, 2013 (updated November 27,

2017), https://www.huffingtonpost.com/2013/09/06/illiteracy-rate_n_3880355.html.

35. Eric A. Hanushek, "Why Can't U.S. Students Compete with the Rest of the World?" *Newsweek*, August 8, 2011, https://www. newsweek.com/why-cant-us-students-compete-rest-world-67213.

36. Josh Zumbrun, "The U.S. May Be the World's Richest Country, but It Ranks 14th in Financial Literacy," *The Wall Street Journal*, November 18, 2015, https://blogs.wsj.com/economics/2015/11/18/ the-u-s-may-be-the-worlds-richest-country-but-it-ranks-14th-in-financial-literacy/.

37. Drickhamer, "Open Book Management."

38. Drickhamer, "Open Book Management."

39. Drickhamer, "Open Book Management."

40. New Belgium Brewing Company, "Rankings," accessed January 31, 2019, https://www.newbelgium.com/brewery/ company/craft-beer-rankings-and-financials.

41. Ann Claire Broughton and Jessica Thomas, "Embracing Open-Book Management to Fuel Employee Engagement and Corporate Sustainability," *UNC Kenan-Flagler* (blog), February 12, 2012, https://blogs.kenan-flagler.unc.edu/2012/02/14/ embracing-open-book-management-to-fuel-employee-engagement-and-corporate-sustainability/.

42. "What We're About," New Belgium Brewing Company, accessed January 31, 2019, https://www.newbelgium.com/brewery/ company/what-were-about. http://www.newbelgium.com/ Brewery/company/what-were-about.

43. Broughton and Thomas, "Embracing Open-Book Management."

44. Donna Fenn, "Show Me the Money: How Four Companies Profit from Open Book Management," CBS News, September 22, 2010, https://www.cbsnews.com/news/show-me-the-money-how-four-companies-profit-from-open-book-management/.

45. "2010 *Inc.* Magazine and Winning Workplaces Recognize Top Small Employers with Exceptional Workplaces," Greenleaf Center for Servant Leadership, June 7, 2010, https://www.greenleaf. org/winning-workplaces/about/press-room/press-release/

inc-magazine-and-winning-workplaces-recognize-top-small-employers-with-exceptional-workplaces/.

46. "About," *A Blog & a Half* (blog), A Yard & a Half Landscaping Cooperative, https://ayardandahalf.wordpress.com/about/.

47. Beaujean, Davidson, and Madge, "'Moment of Truth.'"

Chapter 4

1. *Merriam-Webster*, s.v. "process (*n.*)," accessed December 15, 2018, https://www.merriam-webster.com/dictionary/process.

2. History.com editors, "Ford's Assembly Line Starts Rolling," History, last updated December 13, 2018, http://www.history.com/this-day-in-history/fords-assembly-line-starts-rolling.

3. Amy Gallo, "The Value of Keeping the Right Customers," *Harvard Business Review*, October 29, 2014, https://hbr.org/2014/10/the-value-of-keeping-the-right-customers.

4. Alison Kendrick, "C5 Insight Reveals New Study, Reports Top Factors in CRM Failure," *C5 Insight* (blog), September 24, 2014, https://www.c5insight.com/Resources/Blog/tabid/148/entryid/557/c5-insight-reveals-new-study-reports-top-factors-in-crm-failure.aspx.

5. Direct Marketing News, "63% of CRM Initiatives Fail," July 17, 2013, accessed January 31, 2019, https://www.dmnews.com/customer-experience/news/13059003/63-of-crm-initiatives-fail.

6. *Solution-Chain Manufacturing*, Grant Thornton LLP, 2006.

7. American Hospital Association, "Hospitals Demonstrate Commitment to Quality Improvement," *TrendWatch*, October 2012, https://www.aha.org/system/files/research/reports/tw/12oct-tw-quality.pdf.

8. "The Higgs Boson," CERN, accessed January 31, 2019, https://home.cern/topics/higgs-boson.

9. Carmine Gallo, "How One Brand Builds Customer Loyalty in 10 Feet and 10 Seconds," *Forbes*, July 26, 2012, https://www.forbes.com/sites/carminegallo/2012/07/26/how-one-brand-builds-customer-loyalty-in-10-feet-and-10-seconds/.

10. Taffy Brodesser-Akner, "With Drybar, a Curly-Haired Girl Wages a Global War on Frizz," *The New York Times*, April 25,

2015, https://www.nytimes.com/2015/04/26/business/a-curly-haired-girls-global-war-on-frizz.html.

11. Vanna Le, "How Drybar Went from $1 Million to $70 Million in Just 5 Years," *Inc.*, October 1, 2015, https://www.inc.com/vanna-le/alli-webb-how-a-$70-million-business-blows-away-the-competition.html.

12. Brodesser-Akner, "With Drybar, a Curly-Haired Girl."

13. Clare O'Connor, "How Alli Webb Grew Drybar from Her Backseat to a $70 Million Blowout Chain," *Forbes*, March 8, 2016, https://www.forbes.com/sites/clareoconnor/2016/03/08/how-alli-webb-grew-drybar-from-her-backseat-to-a-70-million-blowout-chain/.

14. O'Connor, "How Alli Webb Grew Drybar."

15. Le, "How Drybar Went from $1 Million to $70 Million."

16. O'Connor, "How Alli Webb Grew Drybar."

17. Amy Farley, "SoulCycle, Casper, and Drybar Execs Reveal the Secrets to Their Cult Brands' Success," *Fast Company*, January 9, 2017, https://www.fastcompany.com/3066369/soulcycle-casper-and-drybar-reveal-the-secrets-of-their.

18. "New Customer-Rage Study Out for Holiday Shopping Season," W.P. Carey School of Business, Arizona State University, November 26, 2013, https://asunow.asu.edu/content/new-customer-rage-study-out-holiday-shopping-season.

19. "New Customer-Rage Study Out," W.P. Carey School of Business.

20. Farley, "SoulCycle, Casper, and Drybar Execs Reveal."

21. "Delivering the Goods," *The Economist*, August 25, 2012, https://www.economist.com/business/2012/08/25/delivering-the-goods.

22. "Delivering the Goods," *The Economist*.

23. "Cleveron Launches CollectNet Parcel Locker Network," *Post&Parcel*, July 18, 2016, https://postandparcel.info/74329/news/cleveron-launches-collectnet-parcel-locker-network/.

24. Kristine Owram, "PUDO Hopes Its Network of Pickup and Dropoff Spots Will Slay Online Shoppers' Persistent Delivery Hassles," *Financial Post*, September 12, 2016,

https://business.financialpost.com/entrepreneur/fp-startups/
pudo-inc-hopes-its-network-of-pickup-dropoff-locations-will-
slay-one-persistent-hassle-for-online-shoppers-delivery.

25. Pick Up. Drop Off. Inc., "PUDO and Retail Council of Canada
('RCC') Working Together to Make Delivery Easier for Retailers
and Their Customers," PUDO, December 6, 2016, http://www.
pudo.ca/investorrelations/news/PUDO%20-%20RCC%20
Dec%2006%202016.pdf.

26. MPI Manufacturing Studies, 2003–2017, The MPI Group.

27. MPI Manufacturing Studies, 2003–2017.

28. Ben Popken, "Zappos Saves Best Man from Going
Barefoot at Wedding," *Consumerist*, May 19,
2011, https://consumerist.com/2011/05/19/
zappos-saves-best-man-from-going-barefoot-at-wedding/.

29. Jim Edwards, "Check Out the Insane Lengths Zappos
Customer Service Reps Will Go To," *Business Insider*,
January 9, 2012, https://www.businessinsider.com/
zappos-customer-service-crm-2012–1.

30. "10 Zappos Stories That Will Change the Way You Look
at Customer Service Forever," *Infinitcontact.com* (blog),
October 29, 2013, https://www.infinitcontact.com/blog/zappos-
stories-that-will-change-the-way-you-look-at-customer-service/.

31. "10 Zappos Stories," *Infinitcontact.com*.

32. Neil Patel, "Tony Hsieh, Zappos, and the Art of Great Company
Culture," NealPatel.com (blog), accessed February 1, 2019,
https://neilpatel.com/blog/zappos-art-of-culture/.

33. Issie Lapowsky, "How ZocDoc Taps the Zappos Approach to
Customer Service," Inc., October 8, 2013, https://www.inc.com/
issie-lapowsky/zocdoc-takes-zappos-approach-customer-service.
html.

34. Lapowsky, "How ZocDoc Taps."

35. Lapowsky, "How ZocDoc Taps."

36. Kimberly Wood, "A Shine on Their Shoes," *BusinessWeek*,
December 4, 2005, https://www.bloomberg.com/news/
articles/2005–12–04/a-shine-on-their-shoes.

37. Patel, "Tony Hsieh, Zappos."

38. Graham Charlton, "Ten Lessons Zappos Can Teach Us about Staff and Customer Retention," *Econsultancy* (blog), July 23, 2014, https://econsultancy.com/ten-lessons-zappos-can-teach-us-about-staff-and-customer-retention/.
39. Jude Stewart, "Zappos CEO Tony Hsieh on Building a Virtuous Business in the City of Sin," *Fast Company*, September 26, 2012, https://www.fastcompany.com/3000839/zappos-ceo-tony-hsieh-on-building-a-virtuous-business-in-the-city-of-sin.
40. Sarah Gaviser Leslie and Jennifer Aaker, "Zappos: Happiness in a Box," Stanford Graduate School of Business (case study), August 23, 2010, https://www.gsb.stanford.edu/faculty-research/case-studies/zappos-happiness-box, p. 3.
41. Bo Burlingham, "The Coolest Small Company in America," *Inc.*, January 1, 2003, https://www.inc.com/magazine/20030101/25036.html.
42. Burlingham, "The Coolest Small Company in America."
43. Anne Claire Broughton, "Zingerman's on Empowering Frontline Staff to Make Better Business Decisions," *Forbes*, December 14, 2016, https://www.forbes.com/sites/thehitachifoundation/2016/12/14/from-beliefs-to-actions-zingermans-on-enabling-better-business-decisions-by-frontline-staff/.
44. Burlingham, "The Coolest Small Company in America."
45. "Forging New Partnerships: How to Thrive in Today's Global Value Chain," National Association of Manufacturers, 2007, http://www.themanufacturinginstitute.org/~/media/98DD408F49194E94B845C4ED456366E5/Forging_New_Partnerships.pdf.
46. National Association of Manufacturers, "The Future Success of Small and Medium Manufacturers: Changes and Policy Issues: Vermeer Manufacturing Works with Customers on Getting Lean," 2006.
47. National Association of Manufacturers, "The Future Success of Small and Medium Manufacturers."
48. National Association of Manufacturers, "The Future Success of Small and Medium Manufacturers."

49. Dave Raffaele, "Social Media Case Study—How JetBlue Used Twitter to Treat Me Like a Human," Dave Raffaele Blog, January 28, 2009, accessed January 31, 2019, via copy available at https://kylesmith341.files.wordpress.com/2010/02/social-media-case-study-how-jetblue-used-twitter-to-treat-me-like-a-human.pdf.

50. JetBlue, 2016 Annual Report, http://blueir.investproductions.com/~/media/Files/J/Jetblue-IR-V2/Annual-Reports/jblu-2016-ar.pdf.

51. Colleen DeBaise, "6 Small Businesses That Are Doing Social Media Right," *Entrepreneur*, July 22, 2013, https://www.entrepreneur.com/article/227392.

52. Franktuary Lawrenceville, "It's always a special moment when a party orders The Last Supper," Facebook, January 30, 2019, https://www.facebook.com/Franktuary/photos/a.10150887246521937/10155924799931937/?type=3&theater.

53. Franktuary (@ Franktuary), "We were proud to contribute to the incredible @strawforward campaign via Sustainable Pittsburgh," Twitter, January 15, 2019, 12:46 p.m., https://twitter.com/Franktuary/status/1085276938749526016.

54. Franktuary, "Want to join our kitchen team?" Instagram, February 1, 2019, https://www.instagram.com/p/BtWYH-VBqwz/.

Chapter 5

1. Gallup, *State of the Global Workplace*, 2017, 4–5, https://www.gallup.com/workplace/238079/state-global-workplace-2017.aspx.

2. Giles Story, "Anticipating Pain Is Worse Than Feeling It," *Harvard Business Review*, March 2014, https://hbr.org/2014/03/anticipating-pain-is-worse-than-feeling-it.

3. Paul R. Lawrence, "How to Deal with Resistance to Change," *Harvard Business Review*, January 1969, https://hbr.org/1969/01/how-to-deal-with-resistance-to-change.

4. Lawrence, "How to Deal with Resistance to Change."

5. Accountemps, "Rumor Has It . . . Office Politics Exist,"

June 29, 2016, http://www.multivu.com/players/
English/7764052-robert-half-accountemps-office-politics/.
6. *Merriam-Webster*, s.v. "politics (*n*.)," accessed December 15, 2018, https://www.merriam-webster.com/dictionary/politics.
7. Polly LaBarre, "The New Face of Office Politics," *Fast Company*, September 30, 1999, https://www.fastcompany.com/37822/new-face-office-politics.
8. Phyllis Korkki, "The Win-Win Way to Play Office Politics," *The New York Times*, November 14, 2008, https://www.nytimes.com/2008/11/16/jobs/16career.html.
9. Arthur Schopenhauer, *Schopenhauer: Parerga and Paralipomena: Short Philosophical Essays, Volume 2*, (Cambridge: Cambridge University Press, 2015), 584–585, Kindle.
10. A.H. Maslow, "A Theory of Human Motivation," *Psychological Review* 50, no.4 (July 1943): 370–396, https://doi.org/10.1037/h0054346.
11. Tomas Chamorro-Premuzic, "The Underlying Psychology of Office Politics," *Harvard Business Review*, December 25, 2014, https://hbr.org/2014/12/the-underlying-psychology-of-office-politics.
12. Warren Bennis, editor's note to *Driven: How Human Nature Shapes Our Choices*, by Paul R. Lawrence and Nitin Nohria (San Francisco, Jossey-Bass, 2002), xiv.
13. Stephen Covey, *The 7 Habits of Highly Effective People*, (Coral Gables, FL: Mango Media), 104, Kindle.
14. "What to Say to a Porcupine: Strategies for Dealing with Difficult Customers," Parature (White Paper), January 2009, p.6, https://docplayer.net/9517069-What-to-say-to-a-porcupine-strategies-for-dealing-with-difficult-customers.html.
15. Jon R. Katzenbach, Ilona Steffen, and Caroline Kronley, "Cultural Change That Sticks," *Harvard Business Review*, July–August 2012, https://hbr.org/2012/07/cultural-change-that-sticks.
16. Katzenbach, Steffen, and Kronley, "Cultural Change That Sticks."
17. Katzenbach, Steffen, and Kronley, "Cultural Change That Sticks."

18. Katzenbach, Steffen, and Kronley, "Cultural Change That Sticks."

19. Barbara Martinez, "Behind Aetna's Turnaround: Small Steps to Pare Cost of Care," *The Wall Street Journal,* August 13, 2004, https://www.wsj.com/articles/SB109234079698090096.

20. Katzenbach, Steffen, and Kronley, "Cultural Change That Sticks."

21. Joel Kotkin, "Grass-Roots Business; Helping the Little Guy Fight the Big Guy," *The New York Times,* October 24, 1999, https://www.nytimes.com/1999/10/24/business/grass-roots-business-helping-the-little-guy-fight-the-big-guy.html.

22. Bob Phibbs, "Marketing: Creating Buzz for Your Small Business [Case Study]," *The Retail Doctor* (blog), April 23, 2015, https://www.retaildoc.com/blog/creating-buzz-for-your-small-business-case-study.

23. Phibbs, "Marketing."

24. Phibbs, "Marketing."

25. John Kenneth Galbraith, *A Contemporary Guide to Economics Peace and Laughter* (London: Andre Déutsch Limited, 1971), page 50, https://archive.org/details/in.ernet.dli.2015.65575/page/n61.

26. Peter F. Drucker, **Management Challenges for the 21st Century** (HarperCollins eBooks, first edition New York: HarperBusiness, 2001), Kindle Edition, location 990.

27. Lawrence, "How to Deal with Resistance to Change."

28. Jack Welch, *Winning: The Ultimate Business How-To Book* (New York: HarperCollins, 2009), Kindle Edition, page 160.

29. Herminia Ibarra, "How Do You Become a Leader?" *Yale Insights,* Yale School of Management, September 30, 2015, https://insights.som.yale.edu/insights/how-do-you-become-leader.

30. Ibarra, "How Do You Become a Leader?"

Afterword

1. Matthew Dickinson, "President Obama: A First-Class Intellect But Second-Class Temperament. Really?," *Christian Science Monitor,* October 28, 2014, https://www.csmonitor.com/USA/

Politics/Politics-Voices/2014/1028/President-Obama-a-first-class-intellect-but-second-class-temperament.-Really.

2. Derek Thompson, "Where Did All the Workers Go? 60 Years of Economic Change in 1 Graph," *The Atlantic*, January 26, 2012, https://www.theatlantic.com/business/archive/2012/01/where-did-all-the-workers-go-60-years-of-economic-change-in-1-graph/252018/.

3. United Nations, "Internet Milestone Reached, as More than 50 Percent Go Online: UN Telecons Agency," *UN News*, December 7, 2018, accessed February 1, 2019, https://news.un.org/en/story/2018/12/1027991.

4. Sara Salinas, "Peak Social? The Major Social Platforms Are Showing a Significant Slowdown in Users," CNBC, August 8, 2018, accessed February 1, 2019, https://www.cnbc.com/2018/08/08/social-media-active-users-around-the-world.html.

5. Paige Cooper, "28 Twitter Statistics All Marketers Need to Know in 2019," Hootsuite, January 16, 2019, accessed February 1, 2019, https://blog.hootsuite.com/twitter-statistics/.

6. US Department of Commerce, Economics and Statistics Administration, Bureau of the Census, "Measuring 50 Years of Economic Change Using the March Current Population Survey," September 1998, https://www.census.gov/prod/3/98pubs/p60–203.pdf.

7. "Welcome to the Post-BRIC World," *The Economist*, May 6, 2013, https://www.economist.com/free-exchange/2013/05/06/welcome-to-the-post-bric-world.

8. "Multipolarity: The New Global Economy," The World Bank, 2011, http://siteresources.worldbank.org/INTGDH/Resources/GDH_CompleteReport2011.pdf.

9. Ernst & Young, "Tracking Global Trends: How Six Key Developments Are Shaping the Business World," May 2011, https://www.eycom.ch/en/Publications/20130129-Tracking-global-trends/download.

10. Mitra Toosi, "Labor Force Projections to 2020: A More Slowly

Growing Workforce," *Monthly Labor Review*, January 2012, https://www.bls.gov/opub/mlr/2012/01/art3full.pdf.

11. Jim Harter and Sangeeta Agrawal, "Many Baby Boomers Reluctant to Retire," Gallup, January 20, 2014, https://news.gallup.com/poll/166952/baby-boomers-reluctant-retire.aspx.

12. Crosby Burns, Kimberly Barton, and Sophia Kerby, "The State of Diversity in Today's Workforce," Center for American Progress, July 12, 2012, https://www.americanprogress.org/issues/economy/reports/2012/07/¹²/11938/the-state-of-diversity-in-todays-workforce/.

13. Arjun Kharpal, "Smartphone market worth $355 billion, with 6 billion devices in circulation by 2020: Report," CNBC, January 17, 2017, https://www.cnbc.com/2017/01/17/6-billion-smartphones-will-be-in-circulation-in-2020-ihs-report.html.
    Global Human Capital Trends 2014: Engaging the 21st-century workforce," Deloitte University Press, 2014, https://www2.deloitte.com/content/dam/Deloitte/ar/Documents/human-capital/arg_hc_global-human-capital-trends-2014_09062014%20(1).pdf.

14. "Global Human Capital Trends 2014," Deloitte University Press.

15. American Psychological Association, "Multitasking: Switching Costs," March 20, 2006, https://www.apa.org/research/action/multitask.aspx.

16. Sharon Begley, "The Science of Making Decisions," *Newsweek*, February 27, 2011, https://www.newsweek.com/science-making-decisions-68627.

17. Begley, "The Science of Making Decisions."

18. "Global Human Capital Trends 2014," Deloitte University Press.

19. "Global Human Capital Trends 2014," Deloitte University Press.

20. Clive Thompson, "End the Tyranny of 24/7 Email," *The New York Times*, August 28, 2014, https://www.nytimes.com/2014/08/29/opinion/end-the-tyranny-of-24–7-email.html.

21. Jeanne Meister, "Social Media: Moving from Danger to Brand Opportunity," *Forbes*, March 26, 2014, https://www.forbes.com/sites/jeannemeister/2014/03/26/social-media-moving-from-danger-to-brand-building-opportunity/.

22. "Global Human Capital Trends 2014," Deloitte University Press.

23. Jessica Brack and Kip Kelly, "Maximizing Millennials in the Workplace," UNC Executive Development, 2012, https://www. kenan-flagler.unc.edu/executive-development/custom-programs/~/ media/files/documents/executive-development/maximizing-millennials-in-the-workplace.pdf.

24. Jacob Morgan, "Why Big Company Doesn't Mean Job Security," *Forbes*, November 14, 2013, https:// www.forbes.com/sites/jacobmorgan/2013/11/14/ why-big-company-doesnt-mean-job-security/.

25. Josh Bersin, "Predictions for 2014: Building a Strong Talent Pipeline for the Global Economic Recovery," Deloitte Development LLC, December 2013, https://www2.deloitte.com/ cn/en/pages/human-capital/articles/predictions-2014-building-strong-talent-pipeline-for-global-economic-recovery.html.

26. Bersin, "Predictions for 2014: Building a Strong Talent Pipeline."

27. Jacquelyn Smith, "Why Your Top Talent is Leaving In 2014, and What It'll Take to Retain Them," *Forbes*, January 24, 2014, https://www.forbes.com/sites/jacquelynsmith/2014/01/24/ why-your-top-talent-is-leaving-in-2014-and-what-itll-take-to-retain-them/.

28. Brack and Kelly, "Maximizing Millennials in the Workplace."

29. Brack and Kelly, "Maximizing Millennials in the Workplace."

30. Bill Vlasic, "U.S. Sets Higher Fuel Efficiency Standards," *The New York Times*, August 28, 2012, https://www.nytimes. com/2012/08/29/business/energy-environment/obama-unveils-tighter-fuel-efficiency-standards.html.

31. Paul A. Eisenstein, "Trump administration moves to revoke Obama-era fuel economy standards," NBC News, August 2, 2018, https://www.nbcnews.com/business/autos/ trump-administration-revokes-obama-era-fuel-economy-standards-n896846.

32. "California Citrus Program," California Department of Food and Agriculture, accessed February 1, 2019, http://www.cdfa.ca.gov/ is/i_&_c/citrus.html.

33. Lynne Duke, "The Man Who Made Kathie Lee Cry," *The*

Washington Post, July 31, 2005, http://www.washingtonpost.
com/wp-dyn/content/article/2005/07/30/AR2005073001413.
html.

34. Gesner Filoso, "Customer Relations Trends to Watch in 2014,"
Sitel, 2013, accessed February 1, 2019, https://www.slideshare.
net/Gesnerf/2014-customer-relations-trends-to-watch-by-gesner-
filoso-sitel-ww.

35. Sara Inés Calderón, "Activists Use Facebook to Help Pressure
Nestlé on Deforestation Issue," *Adweek* (Blog Network),
March 23, 2010, https://www.adweek.com/digital/activists-use-
facebook-to-help-pressure-nestle-on-deforestation-issue/.

36. Jack Newsham, "Market Basket Management Paying for
Missteps in Standoff," *The Boston Globe*, July 22, 2014, https://
www.bostonglobe.com/business/2014/07/21/market-basket-fight-
nightmare/Yi7ilbgSsyrsf3Y4rOBmMK/story.html.

37. Ewan Duncan, Eric Hazan, and Kevin Roche, "Digital
Disruption: Six Consumer Trends and What Businesses Need to
Do Now," McKinsey & Co., March 2014.

About the Author

About the Author

An experienced executive, entrepreneur, journalist,
and researcher, John R. Brandt is the founder and CEO of
The MPI Group, a global management research firm, and the
former editor-in-chief and publisher of both *Chief Executive
and IndustryWeek magazines; he is also the founder and CEO
of Auto(in)correct, a greeting card company. Best known for
groundbreaking research into leadership and performance
excellence across more than fifty thousand organizations while
earning more than twenty editorial awards for excellence, he has
also led more than three hundred advisory, marketing, research,
and data engagements for clients, including Ernst & Young,
Deloitte, Grant Thornton, Infor, the Italian Trade Commission,
Microsoft, Performance Solutions by Milliken, SAP, and many
others. Brandt also maintains a busy lecture schedule, speaking
worldwide on how organizations, industries, and communities
can avoid Nincompoopery and Despair by adapting themselves*

*to the realities of new markets, new corporate structures, and
new customer expectations.*